Discovering Arran

Other titles in this series

Discovering
Arran

ALASTAIR GEMMELL

JOHN DONALD PUBLISHERS LTD
EDINBURGH

ISBN 0 85976 290 4

Phototypesetting by Newtext Composition Ltd., Glasgow.
Printed in Great Britain by Martin's of Berwick Ltd.

Acknowledgements

The Author is most grateful for the helpful co-operation of a number of people and institutions in this project. Dr Andrew Gibb of Glasgow University kindly gave access to a number of papers and documents relating to the island, as did Mr Graham Gemmell of London. Mr John Miller of the *Arran Banner* willingly allowed the author free access to his files and photograph collection. Thanks are also due to Mrs Kay Leiper for drawing the maps.

The *Arran Banner* is thanked for permission to reproduce the illustrations on pages 4, 7, 27, 29, 31, 33, 35, 37, 49, 53, 67, 71, 73, 89, 91, 107, 110, 111, 112, 113, 115, 119, 121, 123, 125, 129, 131, 133, 137, 159, 163, 165, 172, 173, 184 and 185. Graham and Cecile Gemmell gave permission for the illustration on page 99 to be included. All other photographs and illustrations are by the author or from his collection.

Thanks must also be given to the large number of people on Arran, both locals and visitors, who have (often unwittingly) helped the author by the suggestion of ideas or the provision of useful information during the course of many conversations over the years. Although there are far too many of these people to name them all here, the author trusts they will accept his thanks and not feel too slighted if mention is made of only one individual, the late Miss Bess McMillan of Brodick, under whose influence and enthusiasm he was first spurred to start discovering Arran for himself.

Last, but by no means least, the author is happy to acknowledge his wife, June, for her sterling support and encouragement, not to mention proof-reading and the odd glass of whisky when inspiration flagged!

A.G.

Contents

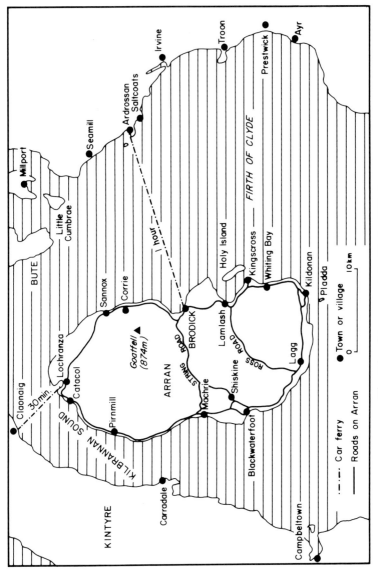

The Isle of Arran and the Firth of Clyde.

CHAPTER 1

Introduction

Would the Firth of Clyde ever have become a focal area for Scottish holidaymakers had the island of Arran not existed? Without its soaring profile gracing the views from the coastlands of Ayrshire westwards across the Firth, there would be little to distinguish that area from, say, the shores of the Firth of Forth. It is the great peaks of Arran which provide that element of grandeur unique to the character of the Clyde. The presence of that wild and contemptuous profile dominating and contrasting with the douce agricultural lowlands and coastlands of Ayrshire has intrigued and inspired artists and poets (though surprisingly enough not Robert Burns) for centuries. Yet he who knows Arran only as a distant profile knows Arran not at all.

As the visitor crowding the rail of the ferry during the crossing from Ardrossan to Brodick soon becomes aware, Arran is a land of far greater complexity than can be imagined from the soft lands of Ayrshire. As the ship draws closer to the island, a myriad of details gradually emerge from the background. The peaks, it is true, seem no less grand as they soar into the clouds or point their weather-torn pinnacles and cliffs to the sky, but the overwhelming severity of their aspect from across the water is gradually revealed as a sham, the mask of distance concealing — rather than lending — enchantment. Contrasts start to become visible — the rich green of farmland along the coast of the island and the little clusters of whitewashed cottages forming the villages of Corrie and Sannox set beneath the dizzying slopes of the northern hills; the brown or purple of the moorlands which fill the southern half of the island and the dark green cloak of the forests which are being planted over nearly a third of the island's area; the cliffs of Holy Island guarding the entrance to Lamlash Bay and the pockets of sandy beaches — adding up to a patchwork landscape of unsurpassed charm.

It is precisely this variety of landscapes that distinguishes Arran from other Scottish islands. By the time the ferry has reached Brodick pier and the passengers have started to disembark, it will already be clear to them that the title bestowed upon the island — Scotland in Miniature — may not be entirely without foundation. All this, and yet they have not seen the half of the variety that is contained within the 165 square miles of the island! The enchantment builds slowly as the visitor becomes more familiar with the island. If, given a fortnight of reasonable weather, the visitor is not hopelessly ensnared by the slow charms of the island, the colour, the romance, the sense of timelessness and of leaving one's troubles behind on the mainland, then they are to be regarded with pity rather than anger or frustration. 'See Naples and die — see Brodick and live!' was the way that one rather over-enthusiastic guidebook of the 1930s expressed the feeling.

The contrasts in Arran can be seen in the comparison of vistas from the ferries which serve the island. Recent developments include the introduction of a service linking Lochranza in the north of Arran with Claonaig on Kintyre. This route has become sufficiently popular to warrant the use of a purpose-built ferry capable of taking 14 vehicles and over 200 passengers across the Kilbrannan Sound to the bare hillsides of Kintyre. Arran, seen from that vantage point, is a stern jumble of jagged peaks and folded hills with the villages of Lochranza and Catacol 'couried-in' under the shadow of the mountains. From this angle there is no sign of the fertile southern half of the island, and the impression is one of almost unrelieved severity.

Further to the south, the hills fall back from the coast to reveal a more open and less intimidating landscape. Particularly in the extreme south the landscape is very exposed, with sheltered spots mainly located where streams come down to the shore. The valleys that these streams flow in are very important aspects of the Arran scene, for the true scenic gems and atmosphere of Arran can only be savoured to the full by leaving the coast and penetrating up some of these glens.

It is in such interior valleys as Glen Craigag or Glen Catacol, far from the intrusive presence of car or house, that visitors can find themselves able to experience true peace and relaxation — the real Arran 'experience'. As you wander along the floor of the glen, with the waterfalls tumbling down the

Goatfell and the other peaks at the northern end of the island rise above the gentle farmland of the Corriegills area, just south-east of Brodick. It is contrasts like this that help to give Arran its unique scenic character.

hillsides around you and the sun glancing across the heathery slopes, while the gulls and curlews cry in the background, it is possible to believe the world to be a place of sublime peace and harmony, imbued with that subtle Celtic melancholy that sadly is lost in the more developed areas around Brodick and Lamlash.

In the peace of the interior and more remote coastlands of the island, it is easy for the imaginative to sit and reflect on the battles fought by the legendary giants and heroes of old — Fingal, Ossian and others of Celtic legend. The tales of their deeds ring round Arran, and those tales underlie much of what is to be felt of the Gaelic influence on the island. These stories effectively link the men with the landscape — the essence of the Celtic tradition. The heroes create the landscape, even sometimes become part of the landscape, and then pass on out of the sight of mortal man, but are themselves immortalised in the landforms and features named after them.

It is not simply the hills and valleys that give Arran its character, but also the interplay of these natural features with the activities of human beings. The location of the island, set almost like a cork in the neck of the Firth of Clyde, has given it

In common with many areas of Scotland in which tourism is a major industry, Arran holds an annual Highland Games in which none of the trappings are spared. Here massed pipe bands, including Arran's own, march and play all the afternoon, providing a memorable sound to accompany the unique sights of such an occasion.

a strong strategic significance, a fact which has played its part in the developing human tapestry since prehistoric times. There is good archaeological support for the idea that among the routes used by the earliest visitors to Scotland after the Ice Age ended about 10,000 years ago, was a west-coast route from the north of Ireland by the short sea crossings to Galloway, Kintyre and Arran before penetrating the central lowlands of Scotland. These early people would have lived a meagre hunter-gatherer existence along the beaches and coastal margins, eating mainly shellfish and fish, though any edible material would have been welcome.

Over the subsequent millennia, the island was to become home for successive waves of settlers until, by the Bronze and Iron Ages, a thriving population had become established, the forests had been partly felled to provide land for agriculture, and pressures and competition for that land were so great as to stimulate the building of a series of defensive strongholds, such as the great fort of Drumadoon, now little more than a single

The sandy beach at Blackwaterfoot is one of the finest on Arran, as this young holidaymaker is discovering.

defensive rampart enclosing an area at the top of a cliff. Later still the early Christian missionaries set up their refuges and monastic foundations among the native population. The location of many of these early religious sites is marked by the presence of a 'kil-' placename, common in parts of the south of the island.

The seas around Arran were later to support the dark sails of the Viking galleys as the island fell under Viking overlordship, being considered part of the Hebrides. It is likely that the longship crews would have been particularly appreciative of the shelter provided by the magnificent harbour of Lamlash Bay, sheltered as it is by the towering crags of Holy Isle. Traces of the Viking influence are still to be found in such placenames as Sannox (Sandvik) and Brodick (Brodvik). The Norse rule ended effectively with the battle of Largs in 1263, after which time the island came within the orbit of the Scottish throne, and castles were built at Brodick, Lochranza and Kildonan.

By virtue of its location, Arran was effectively an area of Hebridean or Highland character and attitudes, but with a nobility that was Lowland Scots in origin and loyalties. Over time, therefore, new ideas came from the mainland, less than twenty miles away, and were applied to the management of the estates on the island, often without regard to the native practices, and not always with any conspicuous degree of success.

The communal farming landscape of the seventeenth and early eighteenth centuries was to be totally altered by the Improvements, in which communal lands were consolidated into compact holdings and the displaced populace forced into other lines of work, such as fishing and kelp harvesting. As was the case in many other parts of the Highlands and Islands at this time, some villages were emptied by forcible eviction of the populace, most of whom were subsequently condemned to emigration to the industrial darklands of Clydeside, or to the new frontiers of eastern Canada, in particular, Megantic County in Quebec.

Traces of all these historical episodes have left their mark on the island if you know where to look. Above all, Arran is not just an island some twenty-six miles from north to south and twelve miles east to west: it is a world of contrasts and of tiny glimpses of past environments and lives. Contrasts exist, particularly between the rock-girt northern peaks and the rolling moorlands and vales of the south, but also between the west with its essentially Hebridean character, and the east where the hotels and boarding houses of the Victorian era proliferate along with the bungalows of modern developments to produce an atmosphere akin to that of the fading but genteel holiday resorts of the mainland.

Contrasts also exist within island society at different times of the year. During the summer months, the island is besieged by visitors, and the natives to some extent 'go to ground', their time and energies being almost wholly devoted to the service of the tourist. Indeed, each month of the season is different from every other month, and has its own band of enthusiasts. Few indeed are the regular August visitors who venture to the island in June or July. Even if they did, it is doubtful if they would feel at home then, for the social make-up of each month's visitors is distinct from that of any other month. For example, May and early June are the season for those with pre-school children, while July and August are the domain of the slightly more mature family — the latter part of August increasingly being the preserve of English visitors as the Scottish schools resume their labours.

Arran was one of the areas of south-west Scotland used as a training
ground during the NATO exercise 'Purple Warrior' in November
1987. Here a group of marines dig in at a vantage point looking across
to Goatfell.

Were any summer visitors to come to the island in winter,
then a total contrast would await them, not just in the colours
of the hills and in the number of people lounging on the
beaches, but also in the social life of the villages. Many of the
local inhabitants only find time to emerge as the tide of
summer visitors ebbs, and they can draw breath once again. It
is considered by many that the true social life of the island only
begins with the departure of the tourists. It is during the winter
that the feeling of a close-knit, self-supporting community is at
its strongest.

The island of Arran repays close acquaintance. Over time,
visitors are likely to become drawn into the fabric of the island,
to become involved in the hopes and aspirations of those who
live there, and ultimately to regard themselves as true
Arranachs. The magical spirit of the island ultimately links all
who have come to love its acres in a common bond. The past
and the present are inextricably intertwined. The future, alas,
is very much more difficult to divine, and is unlikely ever to
appear as romantic as past events viewed through the mystic
glass of the Arran experience.

CHAPTER 2

The Land of Arran

Should the summer visitors to Arran ever come to the island at other times of year, then surprises above and beyond the colder weather will await them. Drive along any of the coastal roads on the island, though the A841 between Brodick and Sannox is the most favoured in this respect, and if it is around Easter, then you can hardly fail to spot flocks of a very important migratory species on the coastal rocks. Distinctive in brightly coloured protective plumage, clusters of geology students are to be found gathered about their tutors or wandering in small groups poking at rock outcrops on the shore. Letters to the local *Arran Banner* have been known to claim first sight of this species in the same way as the early cuckoo is reported in the pages of certain other newspapers, and invest the phenomenon with much the same significance — a harbinger of spring!

Why are the 'geolyboys' (and girls) such regular and numerous visitors to the shores of Arran? Why indeed is it almost impossible to complete an honours degree in geology at a British university without being taken by your tutors for a week or two of concentrated study on the island? The answer, as the late Kenneth Williams was wont to say, 'lies in the soil' — or, to be more exact, in the rocks from which the soil is derived.

Arran possesses such a rich variety of both rocks and landforms squeezed within its confines that it is virtually an exhibition centre for earth scientists. Nowhere else in Britain are so many types and ages of rock found in such a small area, while the contrasts between the mountainous north of the island and the rather more 'douce' terrain of the south allow the geographer and the geomorphologist ample scope for investigations into the sculpting of the earth's surface by the agencies of wind, water and ice.

Lay visitors should not allow the presence of all this academic 'firepower' to put them off. The fact is that in Arran, rocks and landforms are displayed with such clarity that with even a little

The great granite cliffs of Beinn Nuis provide rock climbers with excellent sport. For pilots this mountain has a much less pleasant reputation, as several aeroplanes have crashed into the crags over the years.

knowledge the amateur can easily make exciting discoveries. Indeed, such information can greatly enhance the enjoyment to be had from a ramble along any of the island's glens or coasts. For example, a walk along the north coast of Arran eastwards from Lochranza should include a visit to 'Hutton's Unconformity' (NR 934518), one of the sites at which James Hutton, one of the great Scottish pioneers of modern geology, first identified the geological phenomenon called 'an unconformity'. Visiting the island in 1787, he noted rock strata in schist inclined at an angle in one direction, but overlain by a layer of sandstone with a different inclination. From this relationship, which can still clearly be seen at the site, he concluded that the layers of schist had been tilted and eroded over immense periods of time prior to the deposition of the sandstone, with both rocks subsequently again being tilted away from their previous alignments. This was the first recognition that, over time, layers of rock could be eroded and then fresh layers deposited over them. It dealt a severe blow to the widely held view of that time that all rocks were laid down during the Creation, and laid the foundations for modern geology to invoke periods of thousands of millions of years for the development of the geological patterns visible at the earth's surface.

Indeed, Arran has an honoured place in the history of the science of geology, also being one of the areas in which Hutton gleaned evidence for his theory that some rocks, the so-called 'igneous' rocks, were produced by the cooling of molten magma within the earth's crust rather than all being water-lain as was held by the so-called 'Neptunist' geologists. Hutton's 'Plutonic' theories eventually came to be accepted, and now form the underpinning of modern igneous geology.

Igneous rocks, which include granites and lavas, are widely found in Arran, occupying almost half of the area of the island. These rocks were mainly formed during the so-called 'Tertiary' volcanic episode, some 50–60 million years ago. The landscape would have looked very different then. For a start, it is doubtful that Arran would have been a separate island, but more likely was joined to the mainland. More significantly, the area would have been dominated by an immense volcano, which later collapsed in a form of surface depression or caldera, nearly five kilometres in diameter! The roots of these mighty edifices lie hidden beneath the blanket peat bogs of the moors between the String Road (B880) and the minor road (Ross Road) which crosses the island behind Lamlash, and no trace of them can be seen in the modern topography.

Further north, the breathtaking contours of the northern hills are carved from the remains of another mass of granite, a giant mass of molten magma which pushed its way into the earth's crust some 55 million years ago. The forces involved were so great that the rocks into which this magma was intruded were themselves arched up some 3,000 m. It was the erosion of this cover layer that exposed the granite which has now itself been eroded into the spectacular forms that we see at the present day.

Within the mass of the mountains there are in fact two granites, an older coarse-grained granite into the midst of which a slightly younger, fine-grained granite has been intruded. The coarse-grained granite weathers to give rugged, dramatic scenery, and all the major mountains of north Arran are composed of this rock. Anyone who has puffed his or her way up to the summit of Goatfell will have climbed over or around hundreds of boulders of coarse granite in the upper part of the climb, and can probably testify to the rough texture of that rock and its effect upon the feet during the ascent! The less energetic need not be denied their contact with coarse granite, for it can be seen along the coast road near Corrie in the form of gigantic boulders carried down from the mountains by glacier ice thousands of years ago, and dumped in positions very convenient for the tourist! The two most famous of these boulders are the so-called Cat Stone (NS 020445) and the Rocking Stone (NS 025421), both of which will offer brief diversion to any otherwise unoccupied rock climber.

Sad to say, one must be an altogether hardier soul if the fine-grained granite area is to be explored. It is found mainly in the rather less dramatic rounded hills at the head of Glen Iorsa and Glen Catacol which can only be reached by a somewhat boggy and tedious tramp from the coast road. Again, however, the less adventurous may sample the rock with little more expenditure of energy than a paddle at the mouth of the Iorsa or Catacol Waters, where pebbles and boulders of fine granite are found mixed with other rocks on the bed of the river. Fine granite can be identified by the small size of the crystals making up the rock, and by the pale grey colour of the pebbles.

In the south of Arran, the landscape is dominated by other igneous rocks with a rather different form. These are rocks derived from magmas intruded into the crustal rocks, but with insufficient energy to break through to the surface to form volcanic lavas. Instead, the magma cooled within the crustal rocks, and has only been exposed as a result of the stripping away of the upper layers of the crust by wind and weather. The 'failed' lava flows have two forms, one produced by magma being injected vertically into the crustal rocks to form a narrow sheet, known as a dyke. The other type, called a sill, develops where the magma flowed as an intrusive sheet between the bedding planes of the overlying rock.

The presence of dykes and sills has lent a special character to the south of the island that reinforces the difference between it and the Highland north. The sills, particularly, dominate the scenery. They are usually rather harder than the rocks into which they have been intruded, and over the millennia erosion has worn away those weaker rocks to leave the sills to dominate the terrain. The sills form the steep 'steps' in the landscape that give the hills above Whiting Bay their character, while the massive bulk of Holy Isle (NS 060300), which makes Lamlash Bay one of Britain's finest natural harbours, is also formed from a type of sill known as a cone-sheet, a continuation of which forms the scarp of the Clauchland Hills (NS 030338) which separates the bays of Brodick and Lamlash.

Sills also are the rocks which form the dramatic coastal cliffs at Bennan Head (NR 995203), Dippin Head (NS 050220) and Drumadoon Point (NR 885292). The cliffs at this last site are particularly fine, and can best be admired by wandering along the beach at Blackwaterfoot (or along the golf course, though this is not recommended when the course is busy!) until the point itself is reached. Turning north from here, the middle ground view is dominated by the sill, which here has weathered to form a cliff some 25–30 m high. Note the columnar character of the rock forming the cliff, a function of the way the magma cooled after being injected into the crust.

The last major contribution of the sills to the character of southern Arran is probably the most dramatic, although rather restricted in extent. This is their role in the formation of the waterfalls for which the area is justly renowned. Because the rivers cannot erode the hard sills as rapidly as they can the rock into which they have been intruded, they tend to tumble over the junction between the two rocks in the form of a cascade. Where a sequence of sills crosses the course of a burn, as is the case in Glen Ashdale, a staircase of waterfalls may result. Glen Ashdale Falls (NS 024248), at 40 m the highest in the island, can easily be visited by following signposts pointing up the glen just beside the youth hostel in Whiting Bay (NS 046252) or by following the forestry road reached from South Kiscadale (NS 040254). The forestry road is the easier going, but the path past the youth hostel is probably the more interesting, and leads to a couple of recently constructed viewpoints which allow the falls to be clearly seen.

The more adventurous can see another waterfall produced where a burn tumbles over the edge of a sill in the hills above Kildonan. Eas Mor (NS 020222) can be reached only by

Typical of many of the Arran streams, the North Sannox Water follows a brawling course of alternating pools and rock-girt rapids. In the north of the island the water is crystal-clear where it flows over the granite, but elsewhere the presence of peat often makes the water dark brown.

walking across fields, or if a view from the foot of the fall (whose Gaelic name, the 'Great Fall', reflects its 25 m height) is desired, by struggling through the densely wooded defile above the A841 from the bridge at grid reference NS 020217. This last is very hard going, almost requiring the use of a machete to cut through the undergrowth. It is especially difficult in summer evenings when the dreaded Arran midge is out seeking its prey!

Dykes too have made their distinctive contribution to the character of Arran scenery. In areas where the dyke rock is harder than the rock into which it has been intruded, weathering has often resulted in the dykes forming narrow upstanding walls of rock of a type often blessed by families looking for calm spots to picnic on a windy day! Although dykes are to be found virtually all around the coast of Arran, they are most distinctive on the strip of coast between Brown Head (NR 905240) and Dippin Head (NS 050220). In this relatively restricted stretch of coast over 500 dykes cut across the foreshore. The majority of these dykes are quite small and only reveal their importance in the landscape when viewed from above, as, for example, from the top of the cliffs at Bennan Head, but some, especially near Kildonan (NS 022209), can be up to 8 m high. In this area they form natural breakwaters, and also tend to trap sand so that the coast here is a lovely sequence of little pocket beaches separated by the dark lines of dyke rock.

In the north of the island, the granite itself is cut by a number of dykes. Here, though, it is the granite that is the tougher rock, and the dykes that have been worn away to form the lower ground. Nevertheless, the dykes are still responsible for the development of some of the most interesting and attractive features of the northern mountains. In places, dyke rock has been worn away by rivers to form small gorges, including sections of the Rosa Burn (NR 982480) which contain some lovely pools and waterfalls. Probably the single most distinctive feature attributable to erosion of a dyke is the Witch's Step (NR 977444), a great V-shaped gash in the mountain ridge on the north side of Glen Sannox, which has formed where a dyke cuts across that ridge. This dramatic chasm in the granite cliffs can easily be seen from the Boguille

(NR 973484), the summit area of the Brodick to Lochranza road. Here the great ridges of the northern peaks can be seen rising steeply beyond a moorland foreground, but the eye is continually drawn to the rock pinnacles flanking the 'Step' itself. Whoever the witch was, she must have had a good head for heights, as the traverse of the feature calls for considerable care!

Arran is notable not just for igneous geology, but for a wide range of other rock types. The oldest of these are the ancient schists of north-west Arran, formed more than 500 million years ago, which now underlie the moors and coastal slopes flanking the granite peaks behind Lochranza, Catacol and Pirnmill. Good examples of this rock can be seen in the coastal cliffs and pinnacles at Imachar Point (NR 875405) and along the shore to the west of Lochranza pier, while it forms excellent sunbathing and picnicking platforms alongside the North Sannox Burn where it passes beneath the A841 (NR 993468).

The Dalradian rocks, together with the northern granite, are separated geologically from the rest of the island by part of the Highland Boundary Fault, a great crack in the earth's crust which separated Highland Scotland from the Lowlands of the Midland Valley. In Arran, the fault has no topographical expression, but curves round the granite from the coast north of Lochranza to emerge again at the coast at Dougarie (NR 880372).

To the south of the fault, the predominant rocks are sandstones and conglomerates, with some limestones and beds of coal thrown in for good measure. These sedimentary rocks have weathered to give soils a good deal more fertile than those formed on the igneous and metamorphic rocks, a contrast which is clearly reflected in the greater extent of farmland in the southern half of the island, as well as in the luxuriant woodlands of the more sheltered glens.

Apart from agricultural benefits, the sedimentary rocks were also of more direct benefit to the economy of the island. Both red and white sandstone were quarried in the vicinity of Corrie, and were exported to the mainland, possibly as far afield as Glasgow, for building purposes. Limestone also was dug near Corrie and in the Clauchan Glen, near Shiskine. This stone was burnt to produce lime for use on the fields. Coal was worked in pits near the Cock of Arran in the eighteenth century, where it was used in the production of salt, but no large-scale heavy industry was ever started on the island despite the presence of many of the raw materials which were to be of such value on the mainland during the Industrial Revolution.

Following the emplacement of all these rocks, and the volcanic episodes, earth movements and submergence of the land helped to isolate the island from the Scottish mainland. The date of that isolation is not known, but around the same time large-scale denudation by such agencies as wind and water resulted in the removal of great thicknesses of rock in patterns which were to form the basis of the present-day topography.

One of the most significant of these patterns is the so-called '1,000 ft Platform' which can be seen encircling the northern granite mountains. This platform, a level surface extending over a significant portion of the island, is of uncertain origin. It may be part of a former plain dating from before the island was severed from the mainland. Certainly, large plateaux and moorlands at broadly similar heights are known in Ayrshire, Galloway and Kintyre. It is also suggested that these surfaces may be plains of marine erosion, subsequently lifted to their present position, possibly in a gradual process, with occasional halts in the upward movement. These halts are marked by rather less well-developed platforms cut into the flanks of the hills, for example, behind Lamlash (NS 023294) and at Corriegills where it can be clearly seen in the middle ground of the view towards Goatfell from the South Corriegills Road (NS 036346).

Although the bones of the present topography of Arran, the plateaux, the mountains, the glens radiating from the northern granite and from the central moorlands, formed gradually over a period of many millions of years, a more recent event has left an indelible stamp upon the character of the terrain. The event is the Ice Age, or, to be more exact, the Ice Ages. Over the last 2.4 million years or so, the world has been affected by a series of cold spells, chill enough for glaciers to develop and expand over much of Scandinavia, Britain and northern North America, as well as in major mountain ranges such as the Alps, the Himalayas and the Andes. To date, traces have been found of as many as seventeen such cold spells, the most recent of which ended about 10,000 years ago. In Scotland, however,

The south coast of Arran viewed from the ancient hill fort on Bennan Head, looking eastwards to Kildonan. The line of ancient cliffs, cut when the sea stood at a higher level than the present, is clearly visible, as are the dark lines of the dykes of hard volcanic rock which extend seawards from the coast.

firm proof is only available for the last three or four such cold periods, though there is little reason to doubt that many more have taken place.

On Arran, the impacts of the ice ages are many and varied. At different times, the island was covered by a great ice sheet spreading out from the Scottish Highlands and blanketing the land as far south as South Wales and the English Midlands. The great weight of this ice mass depressed the surface of the land, and as the ice slid over this surface, it rasped and scraped at the rock over which it passed, tearing loose boulders and stones and clay alike, mixing them together and grinding them down to form a stony clay known as 'boulder clay' or 'till'. Thick till deposits can be seen on the island at several locations, especially where streams have cut down into them near Sliddery (NR 940232), in the Clauchan Glen (NR 932300) and where it is exposed in roadside cuttings along the Brodick-Lamlash Road. The ice sheet deposited blocks of the northern granite all over the south of the island, and some blocks were carried further afield, having been found in Ayrshire, Galloway and possibly also in Kintyre.

At times of slightly less intense cold, Arran's mountains were home to a local ice-cap. This ice would have been centred in the northern hills, whence tongues of ice descended, such as in Glen Rosa, Glen Sannox and Glen Catacol. These local glaciers, although small, would still have done a lot of polishing and shaping of the glens and corries. Relics of this time can still be seen in the polished slabs of granite making up the walls of Glen Rosa and Glen Sannox. As the glaciers melted at their snouts, the debris that they were carrying was dropped to form ridges and mounds of material referred to as 'moraines', which mark the positions of those former ice limits. Excellent moraine ridges can be seen at a number of locations on the island, but the best and most easily accessible are to be found in Glen Rosa, where they form a series of mounds on the valley floor (NR 985383) and in the form of a major ridge in Glen Cloy, where the prehistoric fort known as 'Bruce's Castle' (NR 992339) is perched atop a major moraine ridge.

Arran must have been quite a sight in those days. The last period of glaciation to affect the island was about 10,000 years ago. Sea level was relatively high at that time, so the observer standing on the slopes above what is now Brodick pier would have been able to look across the bay to the northern hills and observe that not only were the valleys and corries filled with the white ribbons of small glaciers and snowpatches clustered beneath the dark crags, but that the bay itself was dotted with icebergs which would break off from the snout of the Rosa glacier and slowly and majestically drift out into the Firth of Clyde.

At the same time as ice occupied the more sheltered valleys lying in amongst the high peaks, the peaks themselves were subject to a climatic régime of snow, frost and wind which produced considerable breakdown of the solid rock. The shattered pieces slid or fell downhill to produce extensive screes such as those which blanket the slopes of Beinn Bharrain and Beinn Bhreac behind Pirnmill, or of Holy Isle.

The coastline of the island is fringed by a series of raised shorelines, the formation of which was initiated by events during the glacial period. When the ice masses grew and spread over the land, their weight caused the underlying rock to become depressed rather like the surface of a sponge with a fist pressed into it. The depth of this depression varied according to the thickness of the overlying ice. Once the ice began to melt, the land began to rise again towards its former elevation. This uplift did not take place instantaneously, but gradually, over a period of thousands of years. Indeed, uplift related to the melting of the glaciers over 10,000 years ago is still taking place in parts of Scotland at the present day.

As the ice melted all over the globe, so vast volumes of water which had been 'locked up' in the glaciers were returned to the sea. Sea-level rose rapidly — more rapidly to start with than the land was rising after its release from the yoke of ice — and coastal lowlands became flooded. The coastlines that formed at that time were marked by the formation of beaches and deltas and the cutting of cliffs, exactly as occurs at the present coast, only at a higher level. As the climatic warming ceased, so the rise in sea-level slowed towards a halt while the uplift of the land continued, raising the coastal landforms developed by the high sea-level to a level where they were no longer washed by the sea. This process continued several times, producing a virtual staircase of beaches flanking the shore in some locations, the most notable being around the mouth of the Machrie Water (NR 895335) and Iorsa Water, where the road to the 'Sheepskin Shop' at Auchencar Farm (NR 892367) climbs over a series of raised beaches.

The seas returned to the lands to a minor extent about 5,000 years ago, during a period known as the 'Climatic Optimum' which was rather warmer than present, and during which the extent of glacier melt raised the sea-level slightly higher than it is today. The raised shoreline features associated with these different sea-levels have typical height ranges. The highest ones on the island can be found at heights of about 30 m. Below them, another series of beach sands, etc. can be found in some locations at about 20 to 24 m, while the most extensive raised shoreline, often called the '25-ft beach', can be found at 7 to 10 m above the present sea-level. This shoreline is especially well developed along the coast between Brodick and Corrie, where the road runs for miles along the surface of the beach, while the old cliffline can be seen just inland. The other area where it is most clearly to be seen is the coast between Drumadoon Point (NR 882289) and the mouth of Iorsa Water.

Here, caves, formed by the action of the sea against the cliffs many thousands of years ago, can still be seen, sometimes penetrating the sandstone cliffs to a depth of over 100 feet. The most famous is King's Cave (NR 883310), reputed to have been a hiding place for Robert the Bruce when he began his campaign to attain the Scottish throne.

The result of all these processes of glaciation, erosion, rock formation, etc. over the millions of years has been to produce an island with a physical geography that is varied, complex and fascinating. The larger-scale division between the northern 'Highland' area and the moorlands and hills of the south has already been touched upon, but on a smaller scale great variety is present. Not the least of the attractions of the island is the fact that in a few minutes' driving it is possible to travel through a wide range of types of coastline. Pass from the open coast at Kildonan; around the more verdant inlet of Whiting Bay; over to Lamlash, almost totally enclosed by the protective bulk of Holy Isle; on to Brodick, with the wide sweep of the bay overlooked on the south by the Clauchland hills and the knobbly heights of the Sheeans, and on the north rising to the full majesty of the Goatfell range; and finally to the northern inlet of Lochranza, the water crowded by the hills on both sides to such an extent that the best site for a castle was on a gravel spit protruding into the sea loch; and even the most jaded appetite will have seen at least one coastal vista to enchant and revitalise it.

Lovers of inland water of the flowing variety will find rather more to interest them than lovers of lochs in Arran. Not to put too fine a point on it, most of the Arran lochs are small, inaccessible and rather uninteresting, often with flat boggy margins. Most of them are found on the plateaux and moorlands, the largest being Loch Tanna (NR 920430), reached by a path up from Glen Catacol, which is nearly 2 km in length. Probably the most interesting is Coire Fhionn Lochain (NR 900460), a rock basin occupying a corrie in the granite hills. It is easily reached by a walk of about an hour up a well-marked path from Mid Thundergay (NR 880467), a trek which affords glorious views out over the Kilbrannan Sound to the distant hills of Islay and Jura. The lochan itself is tucked away beneath looming crags, but at both its head and foot there are attractive beaches of whitish-yellow granitic sand. It is a fitting reward for the 'pech' up the hill to the loch to sit in the tranquillity of a sun-bathed beach, a packet of sandwiches in hand and a bottle of some refreshing concoction cooling quietly in the clear waters. The sense of peace, achievement and well-being is hard to match.

Two of the Arran lochs are rather curious. Loch na Davie (NR 950458) is little more than a small shallow pond dotted with boulders, but is notable for having two streams drain from it — the Easan Biorach to the north and the Iorsa Water to the south! Similarly shallow, but at a much lower altitude, Loch a'Mhuillin (NR 940496) near Lochranza is even more curious. It is only about 15 m above sea level, and is ponded up by a ridge of presumably glacial origin, possibly augmented by human agency. Its name, which means 'Loch of the Mill', suggests that it may have provided water to drive a mill-wheel in the past. At present, it is notable for the boggy nature of its margins. Indeed, it is difficult to know just where the margins are, for there are mats of floating vegetation close to the shore, and unwary persons may venture some distance out into the loch before the spongy feel of the ground as they step on it alerts them to potential problems!

The rivers and streams of Arran are among its particular attractions. None is especially long, the majority in the north of the island radiating outwards from the northern granite hills, while in the south the longer rivers flow towards the west coast. The longest river, the Iorsa Water, is only about ten miles long, while the majority of streams in the north will be less than five miles long. What they lack in size is more than compensated for in character, the burns progressing down the steep slopes in sequences of cascades and pools. The clarity of the water draining from the granitic slopes makes many of the pools most attractive places for the hiker to cool weary feet (or more!). In some locations, streams flow over polished slabs of granite like liquid curtains, twitching with the fluctuations of the flow and trailing their hems in the cool stillness of the pools. Such slabs form favourite spots for picnics in many of the glens, with those in Glen Rosa being especially commended.

In the south of the island the streams have a rather different character. The peat-covered moorland sources of most of these rivers yield a dark-brown water, particularly so after heavy rain. The streams draining west from the moors tend to flow in narrow valleys which open out somewhat as they approach the coast. Many of those flowing to the south coast flow in shallow valleys interrupted by waterfalls as they cascade over some of the sills described earlier. To the east, the streams in valleys such as Glen Cloy and the Benlister Glen descend quite steeply from the moorlands in a series of cascades, but then flow quite gently towards the sea.

These southern streams are less well known than those in the north of the island, and often seem less enticing in character. They are nevertheless well worth a closer look, as attractive pools and gorges where ferns and trees overhang the water, creating a verdant, shaded environment more interesting to the fisherman and naturalist than to the sunbather.

There is much in the land of Arran to attract the collector, both amateur and professional. Fossil shells have been collected from caves in the limestone behind the old harbour in Corrie. These caves, largely formed by the quarrying of limestone, have not been used for some time, and are dangerous. Even quite recently, rescuers have had to be called out to extract the unwary from their grasp, and it is best to avoid them, no matter how enticing they look. The enthusiastic fossil-hound can much more safely be indulged by a walk along the foreshore at Corrie.

The mineralogist also can pick up examples of various types of quartz, even some smoky quartz, beryl and topaz, in fissures in the granite of the northern hills, and can also look for traces of barytes in Glen Sannox, where it was formerly mined and exported widely for use in industry.

It must be emphasised that Arran is an almost unique natural museum of geology, and as such needs conservation. The thousands of students who visit it each year are (for the most part) carefully controlled and forbidden to remove material from the most famous sites. It would be nice to think that the casual visitor likewise could be persuaded to refrain from exporting the island in a million small samples, and leave something for future generations to admire. The collector of landscapes, who puts the scenes that typify the island onto film for future use, sets an example that others would be well advised to copy if the wonders of the island are to be preserved.

CHAPTER 3

The Natural Environment

'Arran of the many stags . . . skittish deer are on her pinnacles, soft blackberries upon her waving heather . . . in all her glades a faultless grass . . . smooth were her level spots — her wild swine they were fat . . . under her rivers' brinks trout lie; the seagulls wheeling round her grand cliffs answer one the other — at every fitting time delectable is Arran!' This quotation from the 'Lay of Arran' by Caeilte, the ancient Ossianic bard, indicates that the variety and fertility of the island have long been reflected in the range of flora and fauna that it can support. It must truly have been a source of rich harvests and good hunting in days gone by, and still retains some of that character even to the present day. The keen amateur naturalist need have no fears of being bored on Arran!

The end of the glacial period would have been greeted on Arran by an essentially barren landscape, save for some hardy tundra plants and shrubs, such as mosses, dwarf birch and dwarf willow, that could withstand the extremes of climate prevalent at that time. Over the following thousands of years, the island has been subjected to fluctuations of that climate, and in response to those ups and downs of temperature and rainfall, plants, birds and animals have migrated to the island, some to thrive, others to die out.

The melting of the glaciers was not brought about by a major warming of the climate, but rather by a gentle rise in temperature, so the environment was still cold and wet at that time. During the next couple of thousand years, a warming and drying of the climate affected all of Britain, and trees began to spread into the island, colonising the coastal areas and the sheltered glens, and slowly spreading up the hills onto the moorlands. By five to six thousand years ago, the treeline was rather higher than it is at present, and most of the island would have been covered in dense forest, mixed deciduous forest with oak and hazel on the low ground, but at altitude probably pine mixed in as well.

The climate continued warm, but became wetter about 5,000

years ago, coinciding with the short-lived rise in relative sea-level during the 'Climatic Optimum' phase. The increased wetness gave conditions ideal for the formation and growth of peat bogs in the upland moors, as well as on some areas of poorly drained low ground. Thereafter the climate again became cooler and dryer, leading, about 2,500 years ago, to the adjustment to the mild wet climate that we know today.

We are able to gain some idea of the environment and vegetation of these past times through the analysis of plant remains which have been preserved in peat bogs and in the muds and oozes on the beds of lochs. By looking at the changing patterns of plant remains and pollen grains in the various layers, a picture can be built up of the fluctuations in vegetation which have accompanied the climatic changes. Evidence of this sort on Arran has been derived from two main locations, Machrie Moor on the west coast (NR 910323), and Loch a'Mhuillinn at Lochranza. A comparison of the two sites, one in the 'Highland' part of the island and the other in the 'Lowland' area, shows that Arran justified its image of 'Scotland in miniature' throughout the period in question.

The tale revealed by the scientific study of the two sites starts with a slow period of recovery from the widespread impact of the glaciers. Over the whole island, about 10,000 years ago, there was little or nothing in the way of vegetation to soften the bleakness of the scene. Amongst the bare rocks and the snowpatches would have been a vegetation very like that found in the high Arctic at the present day — just a few lichens and the occasional dwarf willow or birch to relieve the monotony. This early vegetation is likely to have grown from seeds blown onto the island by the wind, or carried there by birds from the mainland or from Northern Ireland.

As the centuries passed, the plant cover slowly increased, both in extent and variety, aided by the gradual warming of the climate. The early willow, birch and juniper forest became restricted to the high hills, while the lowlands and the glens saw the flourishing of a much lighter woodland, including hazel, oak and elm, with alder and willow dominating the damper patches in the poorly-drained valley soils.

Charcoal fragments from Machrie Moor indicate that the first human influence on the island may be as much as 8,500

Spring snow still lies in the gullies of Beinn Tarsuinn as it rises majestically from the moorlands.

years old, more or less the same time as the beginning of the development of the deciduous forest. It has even been suggested that hazel and oak may first have been brought to the island in the form of nuts and acorns collected on the mainland for food by these early nomadic peoples.

Later, as the climate became warmer, primitive agriculture — probably based initially on the 'slash and burn' principle still practised by native tribes in areas like the Amazon basin and parts of New Guinea — seems to have become established. Each family or tribal group would hack out a clearing in the forest, burn the trees and use the ash to fertilise the soil. They would grow their crops until the soil was exhausted, then move on and begin again at a new location. The effects of this way of life can be seen in the decline in fossil remains associated with trees, and the increase in traces of grasses, weeds and herbs. In the Machrie Moor area, cereal grains have been found dating from about 5,300 years ago. In contrast, the site at Lochranza shows little trace of significant human presence much before 4,000 years ago. Presumably the greater fertility and friendlier environment of the south proved more of an attraction to the very early settlers than the colder, more austere northern valleys of Arran.

The relative impacts of human activity in the north and south of the island can be seen in the fact that about 5,000 years ago, forest trees contributed over 70 per cent of all the pollen grains falling into Loch a'Mhuillinn, when in the mires and ponds on Machrie Moor similar trees contributed only 45 per cent of the pollen. Forest clearance was thus both earlier and more extensive in the southern half of the island.

Following this period, it is likely that the vegetation in Arran was affected greatly by human activity. Tree clearing, planting of crops, pastoral activity, the burning of moorland, and other actions related to primitive agriculture, have left scars on the vegetational history of Arran that are so deep as to indicate that for the past 5,000 years, the island has not had a truly natural environment. A number of the chambered cairns built by these early agriculturalists can still be seen on the island, as, for example, at Moss Farm (NR 907324) and at Torbeg (NR 903311) near Machrie Moor.

Following the 'Climatic Optimum', wetter and somewhat cooler conditions promoted the spread of heather and the growth of peat on both high ground and ill-drained lowlands. Cereal production declined, and by about 4,000 years ago increasing soil acidity was beginning to be a problem for the early farmers. Put this together with the miserable, wet and windy conditions that prevailed in Arran at that time, and it is hardly surprising that the extent of 'farming' at that time was very limited.

These early Arranachs were not completely at the mercy of the whims of nature. They knew something of husbandry and soil fertility, and about 2,200 years ago some enterprising local is known to have spread shell sand onto peaty soils, presumably to improve fertility, in just the same way as the modern farmer will lime a field. These improvements were necessary as conditions throughout the late Bronze Age and Early Iron Age, even through the Dark Ages (up until about A.D. 700), made agriculture difficult in Arran, and it was not until around the time of the Vikings that signs of significant increases in human activity on the land took place.

Even at the present day, agriculture in parts of the west of Arran is highly marginal, and is almost totally confined to the coastal lowlands. It is only in the milder and more sheltered

Some peat is still cut even today from the peat-beds at the top of the Boguillie, the pass between Lochranza and Sannox.

eastern glens and bays, and in areas of the south, sheltered from westerly gales, that the moorlands and peat have been driven back to any great extent from the coast. Even there, some of the marginal hill farms are being abandoned or amalgamated, their owners beaten by a combination of economics and weather.

The fact that the plant and animal life of the island has been significantly affected by human activity should not put off the nature-lover who wishes to come to Arran. Despite all that has been said about the island, it supports a very extensive wildlife. The mountains, rivers, moors and coasts provide a whole variety of environments for plants, animals and birdlife, and the ornithologist whose binoculars have been forgotten when packing to go on holiday will be sad indeed. The islanders themselves have a flourishing Natural History Society whose members are treated to a varied programme of walks and lectures about Arran by visiting and local experts. Wildlife is also becoming a recognised aspect of tourist promotions.

Recent developments on the island include such activity holidays as bird-watching and flower-spotting walks and tours.

The Climate of the Island

One of the reasons why Arran supports a very varied range of plants and animals is the climate. No one who knows the island would deny that it has very variable weather, but if asked to suggest a phrase that might sum it up, the words 'mild and damp' spring readily to mind. This is not to deny warm, dry weather in summer, but even then the chances of getting a two- or three-week holiday without having a couple of wet days are very slim.

It would be silly to claim that Arran is 'Scotland in miniature' in respect of its climate — there is no area with a climate like that of the north-east of Scotland, for example — but the island does display a surprising degree of variation of weather within its bounds. It is far from uncommon for it to be raining heavily for much of the day in the north-west of the island, while the Whiting Bay area sees nothing but sun with occasional clouds at that time! There is also a variation in weather with altitude, as many of the ill-prepared trippers who venture onto the slopes of Goatfell clad only in shorts, T-shirt and sandals will find to their cost if they ever manage to reach the summit!

Mild, wet winds, blowing in from the Atlantic, bring much of the rain to Arran. As this air meets the barrier of the Arran hills it is forced upwards and is cooled. Water condenses out of water vapour, and falls as rain or snow on these upland areas. The average fall at Dougrie (NR 882372) is only about 1,150 mm (46 inches) per annum, but across in Brodick, which is really still within the hills, it is as much as 1,750 mm (70 inches) per annum. In the hills themselves, the falls must be even greater.

In the winter, the average temperature may be as low as 2 to 3 °C, but heavy frosts are rare, as are periods of prolonged snowfall at low altitudes. Even the high peaks will not keep a snow cover continuously throughout the winter, while at lower altitude snow is unlikely to lie for more than a day or two. Despite this, Arran roads become as chaotic as those anywhere

Although generally blessed with a mild winter climate, Arran motorists are as liable as those anywhere else to have problems when it snows.

else in Britain during a blizzard. A few years ago a Post Office Land Rover had to be abandoned by its driver at the top of the String Road as a result of running into a snowdrift. However, Arran is not a place for skiers, and its winter climate is more noted for mildness than severity.

In summer, average temperatures are 16 to 17 °C, with the driest periods tending to be early summer (May/June) with another good spell often occurring in September. During spells of hot anticyclonic weather in summer, some of the more sheltered glens may become almost too hot for comfort if they are protected from the influence of a cooling breeze. Rather more common, though, is the light 'smirr' or drizzle which drifts with the wind and seems able to penetrate all but the most impervious waterproofs. Although periods of drought have been known quite recently in Arran, with the grass on the golf courses being burnt brown, the more common situation is a fine balance between wet and warmth. In some of the glens in the hills, the wetness of the climate has promoted a boggy vegetation which covers the valley floor, so that even in a dry spell it is often virtually impossible to go for a walk into the mountains and emerge dryshod unless wearing boots. In wet weather, even boots may not prove adequate protection. One old guide to the island advised walkers to start any hike by finding a stream and paddling in it until they got water in their boots, thereby saving themselves the worry for the rest of the day as to whether or not they were going to get their feet wet!

In terms of plant growth, probably the most significant aspect of the climate is neither temperature nor rainfall, but wind. Although the westerly wind is the most common, and can blow quite fiercely on occasion, gales come more commonly from the north-west or the south-east. Particularly on the western side of the island, the frequency and force of winds has a huge impact on the vegetation. Trees in exposed areas grow in strange shapes because of the effect called wind-pruning, where the wind inhibits the growth on the exposed side of the tree, but on the more sheltered side growth is relatively normal. This gives rise to the impression that the trees are often hunched, crouching into the hillsides to avoid the worst effects of the wind.

The impact that the wind can have is best demonstrated by visiting a really sheltered area, and looking at the contrast in vegetation compared with the more exposed parts of the island. In areas such as Lagg (NR 955216) and the famous gardens at Brodick Castle (now owned by the National Trust for Scotland), plants grow in profusion. Trees are tall and straight, flowers flourish and bloom for much of the year, and the impression is almost of a jungle held in check.

The 'jungle' analogy is strengthened by the types of plants which grow there. In the sheltered areas, the mildness of the climate allows a wide range of rhododendrons to grow in the open, including some species that have to be grown under glass in most parts of Britain, not to mention various gum trees, palm trees and other exotica, although many of the palm trees on the island are not true palms but rather palm lilies. True palms from places such as China and the Mediterranean were successfully grown at Cromla, a house in Corrie where the Revd Dr David Landsborough, a noted nineteenth-century naturalist and traveller, used to come with his family to stay with a relative and sometimes brought back specimens to try

The numbers of red deer in the north of the island are now such that older stags such as this one can safely be culled by the keepers to allow the younger and more vital stags access to the hinds without endangering the viability of the herds.

and grow in the mild environment.

And so, as you travel around the island, or walk in the interior, you are likely to become aware of changes in the types of plants and animals from place to place. These very different environments provide a rich harvest for the dedicated naturalist, but a pretty substantial yield too for those with a little knowledge who simply keep their eyes open as they go about their various chosen activities on the island.

The Coasts

The coastline of Arran is one of ever-changing habitats for plants and animals. Some parts, as around Bennan Head (NR 992203), have cliffs overlooking the sea. Here fulmar and kittiwake are known to nest, ravens and carrion crows are seen, and hawks such as the peregrine falcon eke out an existence by preying on the seabirds. Plants such as sea plantain and red campion grow on such cliffs, as do trees such as rowan and hazel in those places where there is still some moisture on the cliff.

Much of the coast is flat, fringed by raised beaches which are often backed inland by fossil cliffs, marking the position of a former sea-level. The actual shoreline along such coasts can be rocky, with many pools and little promontories, as can be seen from the A841 between the Old Pier at Brodick Castle and Sannox. In places the rocky nature of the shore may be hidden beneath a blanket of shingle, though this is more common on the west coast. Here the pebbles may become piled up by storm waves into definite ridges such as those that can be seen from the A841 just west of the pier at Lochranza (NR 920509) and south of Imachar Point (NR 865400). Sometimes the shingle gives way to sand which has become trapped in little bays and pockets in the coast. Very pleasant beaches have formed in such places as Kildonan (NS 035207), where the sand is reached by a flight of steps down a cliff virtually beside the coastguard station, Pirnmill (NR 867428), where sand is exposed at low tide, and the little bay (NS 019389) near the main entrance for cars to the grounds of Brodick Castle.

The raised beaches, where covered in shingle, are quite well-drained and in some parts of the island are used for a narrow strip of pasture between the sea and the fossil cliffs. Where the coastal strip is not cultivated, then heather, bracken and whins form the dominant cover. When they are in bloom, the perfume from the whins is the first thing to strike you as you approach. Elsewhere, the raised beach is underlain either by glacial boulder clays or, more commonly, by bedrock close to the surface. This type of situation is found in many areas, such as the coast between Merkland Point (NS 027388) and Corrie, and unless artificial drainage has been installed will give rise to rather damp conditions in which rushes, lilies and sphagnum moss grow well, often interspersed with patches of alder. Flowers seen here may include marsh marigold, irises and lesser celandine, while thrift, thyme and stonecrop are among the plants to be found on the rocky outcrops on the coast itself.

More extensive sandy beaches, backed in some cases by limited development of dunes, can be seen at Brodick, Sannox, Machrie and Blackwaterfoot, the last being the best-developed example. At Brodick erosion of the beach, attributed by many

In the drier months of summer small fires can easily start, threatening plantations of young trees, especially if the peaty soils they are planted in ignite. Here a small peat fire in the south of the island is being kept under close control.

to exploitation of the sand supply for export, is not only threatening the golf course which runs along the coast, but also the use of the beach by tourists. On these sandy coasts, the dunes are often backed by a sandy plain, covered in short grasses, forming a lovely natural springy turf, called 'machair' in the Gaelic. The name 'Machrie' is presumably derived from this word.

While a range of finches and warblers inhabit the wetter parts of the coastal strip, for the ornithologist the true interest lies in the actual sea edge and inshore waters. At the fringe of the water, waders and plovers can be seen going busily about their chores. Greenshank, redshank, sandpiper, bar-tailed godwit, dunlin, golden plover, ringed plover and turnstone are among the other coastal species which have been recorded on Arran. The commonest of all is the almost ubiquitous oystercatcher or sea-pyat, whose black and white body, long orange beak, rapid flight and sharp cries make it difficult to ignore on any walk along the shoreline.

Rather more stately coastal birds include the curlew, with its

distinctive curved beak, and the heron, often seen fishing along
the coast or in inland rivers. It stands as a grey and lofty
sentinel in the pools and shallows, being particularly common
along the coast between Brodick and Corrie. There is still a
heronry in the Castle Woods at Brodick, despite an old legend
that when the herons left, the Dukes of Hamilton would leave
the castle. The Hamiltons have now gone, but it seems the
herons are made of sterner stuff!

A common sight along the coastal strip is an offshore
boulder acting as a stage upon which cormorants and shags
stand, often with wings widespread. In the waters round about
gulls of all varieties bob or fly overhead. Herring gulls, black-
headed gulls and greater and lesser black-backed gulls are seen
frequently and in considerable numbers, filling the air with
their cries and their squabbling behaviour.

The range of ducks to be seen floating in the sea around the
coast is very impressive. Driving between Brodick and Corrie,
at times it seems that almost every inlet in the rocky coast is
playing host to mallard, shelduck or a family of eider duck.
Other species to be spotted by the keen observer include
shoveller, teal and red-breasted merganser, while in winter
scoter, pochard, wigeon and golden-eye are among the
seasonal visitors. The mixture is further enhanced by the
occasional sighting of grebes, great northern, black-throated
and red-throated divers, arctic terns, and black guillemot.
Gannets, probably from the great gannetry at Ailsa Craig, are
often seen patrolling the coastal waters off Corrie and in the
Kilbrannan Sound. There can be few more thrilling sights in
ornithology than to see a group of these great white birds
fishing off the Corrie shore, flying up to thirty metres above
the water before folding their wings and plunging into the sea,
beak outstretched, to emerge a few seconds later with a fish.

Fish are plentiful in these waters. Cod, whiting, mackerel and
haddock are common, while saithe and pollack can be found
on rocky coasts, and flounders are seen in the sandy bays.
Indeed sea angling has been so good that it has formed the
basis for a festival at Lamlash for a number of years now. As is
the case in seas all over the world, overfishing seems to be
causing some problems, and the 1987 festival produced very
poor catches. The 1988 results were better and hold promise
for the future continuance of the festival.

Seals basking on the rocks around the coast of Arran were a common sight until the seal virus of the late 1980s killed a number of them. Happily the damage to the seal population was not too extensive, and numbers are now showing signs of rising again.

The range of fish is less than it was a hundred years ago. Records of the mid-nineteenth century talk of catches including skate, sole and turbot, which are seldom caught nowadays. Legend has it that Lochranza was also noted at that time for its oysters — a delicacy that sadly is no longer produced on the island.

Of the larger sea creatures, although porpoises can be seen on occasions around the coast, and seals are found in many parts of the coast, basking on the rocks at low tide or bobbing about in the waves, probably the most spectacular inhabitant of the waters of the Firth of Clyde is the basking shark, which can be seen most summers as a black dorsal fin cutting slowly through the water in best 'Jaws' style! There the resemblance ends, for the basking shark is a plankton eater (consuming up to half a ton a day!) which grows to fifteen metres in length and is a true 'gentle giant', posing not the slightest danger to bathers or small boats. The much smaller and rather more vicious thresher shark can also be seen, but very rarely, from shoreline vantage points.

Low Ground and Pasture

Most of the agricultural land in Arran is low-lying and well-protected from the wind, though the largest lowland of all, the valley from Machrie extending past Shiskine (NR 912298) to Blackwaterfoot, is open to the westerly gales, as are the pastures of the south end of the island which extend up to 150 m above sea level. Most of the patches of deciduous and mixed woodland on the island are found on low ground where there is shelter from these westerly winds. The mountains screen the area around Brodick Bay, and particularly around the castle and estate policies, from such winds, allowing the development of a very well-wooded aspect. Oak, ash, hawthorn, hazel, alder and willow grow in these areas as well as on the mountain and moorland slopes, but chestnut, elm, lime, Scots pine, beech and sycamore also flourish in artificially planted situations.

Hawthorn hedges divide the fields in the southern part of the island, and can also be found in the north in those areas where the wind is not too fierce or the soil too thin. In May and early June, the profusion of white blossom on these hedges adds greatly to the character of many of the minor byways of the island. Further colour is added in the villages and around some of the farmhouses by hedges of fuchsias which provide vivid shades of red in summer. Elsewhere on the island dry-stone dykes are used to mark boundaries between fields, giving a rather more austere tone to the landscape.

The more cultivated landscapes play host to a wide selection of birdlife ranging from nightjars, treecreepers and long-tailed tits (in the woods by Brodick Castle) to a range of finches, warblers, thrushes, wagtails, whinchat and other small birds in gardens, hedges and orchards. The corncrake has been heard around Shiskine, and it is thought that it may be trying to re-establish itself after becoming virtually extinct on the island. The cuckoo is a common visitor, tending to use meadow pipit, hedge sparrow and robin as the preferred host species for its young. The barn owl breeds on the island, as does the short-eared owl, the latter being a creature of the forestry plantations. Kestrel, sparrowhawk and buzzard patrol the hedgerows and the verges of the roads on the lookout for small mammals.

OFFICIAL
NATURIST BEACH

Beyond this notice
clothing need not be worn
for bathing, sunbathing
or other recreation

A tourist development which did not meet with universal approval among the local inhabitants was the designation of a beach at Cleats, near Lagg, as the first naturist facility on the island. The sign erected there, modelled here by two of the girls from the Isle of Arran Tourist Board, gave rise to some startled comment when it first appeared, though the furore has died down now.

Seasonal visitors abound. In summer the skies are full of the darting streamlined forms of swallows and house-martins. Sand-martins have been recorded as nesting in sandy riverbank sites in the west of the island, but the swift is rarely seen. In winter, fields may be full of the honking forms of migrant greylag geese.

If very lucky, the visitor may catch a glimpse of the wonderful blue and orange blur that is a kingfisher, speeding about on a fishing trip along one of the burns. Glen Rosa is the place to spot these elusive birds. The rivers are also fished by heron, presumably looking for sea trout, or possibly even a small salmon. In the smaller burns, the characteristic white breast and bobbing movements of the dipper can be seen, the bird often rushing into the water in search of food.

It is feared that the dipper, together with quite a number of other birds and animals, has had its numbers reduced as a result of being hunted by mink. Arran has few predatory

mammals, the stoat, the weasel, the polecat, the fox and the
wildcat not being found on the island. When a farmer released
some mink a few years ago, they had no natural competition
except for a few otters, and were able to flourish in the wild.
Some otters are still found on Arran on the quieter rivers, but
mink have spread over virtually the whole island, becoming a
major pest in the process by taking chickens from farms.

In the woods around Brodick, the red squirrel can still be
seen scampering around the trees. The grey squirrel, usually
the scourge of its red cousin, is unknown on the island and the
red squirrel, itself a relatively recent import, flourishes. Of the
other native mammals, badgers are rarely seen but do exist,
while hedgehogs, rabbits, hares, shrews, mice and voles are
common, as unfortunately is the rather less attractive brown
rat. A parish record of 1845, mentions the former presence of
roe deer and wild boar in the forests of Arran, but these
potentially exotic inhabitants of the forests have long departed
the local scene.

Mountain and Moorland

The largest part of the island is occupied by mountain and
moorland, though the moors in particular are gradually being
taken over by the dead hand of afforestation which is slowly
smothering them in a dull green carpet of spruce and larch.
Before the coming of the forester, trees in upland areas
consisted largely of small clumps of rowan and birch, plus one
rather more unusual tree, the whitebeam (*Sorbus*), a relative of
the rowan. Whitebeam grows on Holy Isle (NS 050300) and in
Gleann Diomhainn (NR 925467) where two varieties of *Sorbus*
grow, clinging to the walls of a rocky gorge. The particular
interest of these trees is that these species are among the rarest
trees in Scotland, so they are protected in a little nature reserve
in Gleann Doimhain. The Nature Conservancy erected a fence
around the site, but provide information boards to help the
visitor identify the plants.

The natural moorlands are covered with heather or with
peat hags on the less well-drained plateau areas. Bracken is
often found on the slopes leading down from the moors

towards the glens, while reeds and bog cotton fringe the lochs and small bog areas up on the plateau. Wet areas, especially near the sources of streams, often house thick spongy growths of sphagnum moss. Bog myrtle is another plant of the damper glens and moorland. Crushing the leaves and rubbing them between the fingers releases a refreshing aroma which can serve as a brief pick-me-up to the weary hiker.

In the west and south of the island in particular, huge tracts of moorland are being taken over by afforestation, in total affecting almost a third of the island. Many of these plantations have been started within the past 25 years, so that the adjustment of plants and animals to the new environment is not complete. These changes mean that a number of the moorland and peatland plants and animals are found nowadays in a much more restricted area than was formerly the case. It would be tragic if the spread of trees led to the loss of one of the characteristic environments of Arran, the moorlands. The island may be in danger of losing its 'Scotland in miniature' tag unless care is taken to maintain the variety of its ecological environments.

By climbing from the moors onto the mountains, gradually the wetland plants are left behind. As you climb higher, first of all the heather begins to thin, and then, as the high corries are reached and the peaks and ridges approached, short grasses, mosses and lichens, together with willow and a range of succulent berries, including cloudberry and crowberry, form the main vegetation. The tops themselves show a lot of bare rock and granite gravel, but a thin turf has developed on some of the summit plateaux, especially on Beinn Tarsuinn (NR 959412), Caisteal Abhail (NR 968443) and Mullach Buidhe (NR 995430).

These moorlands and mountains are home to an extensive and exciting range of bird and animal life. Meadow pipits, larks, stonechat, whinchat and wheatear inhabit the moorlands, and may be preyed upon by the merlin, seen on rare occasions on the island, or by the hen harrier. Both curlew and whimbrel are found, the former with its mournful cry almost like an expression of the loneliness of the moors in which it lives. Higher up toward the first slopes of the mountains the ring ouzel breed and the dotterel is a rare visitor.

The fringes of the moorland lochs are nesting grounds for large numbers of gulls in summer, while the red-throated diver has been known to nest at the Urie Loch (NS 002280), though its numbers may have been affected by attacks on eggs and chicks by gulls, mink and crows. Hooded crows and jackdaws are found in considerable numbers around the fringes of the moorland, while the much larger shape of the raven can be seen in the skies over the island, their loud croaking often announcing their presence even when they cannot be seen in the clouds.

Game birds are becoming much scarcer than formerly. Woodcock, snipe and black grouse used to be found in the north of the island in numbers, but are rare now. The ptarmigan, a bird of the high tops, was common in the eighteenth and nineteenth centuries, but there are no records of sightings in the twentieth century before 1973. Occasional sightings are now recorded from the northern peaks, and the bird seems to be making something of a comeback on the island. Red grouse, the main game bird on the island, are much more common, as the hiker who inadvertently sets the bird off from beneath his feet in a startling explosion of noise and movement will be able to confirm. In 1912, the bag of grouse was nearly 13,000 birds, but in the 1940s disease caused a major decline in numbers which have not yet fully recovered their previous levels. Pheasant and partridge have been introduced to the island as game birds, but are less numerous and tend to inhabit the lower woodlands and fields.

Probably the pride of Arran birdlife is the golden eagle, of which there are at least two pairs known on the island. Their majestic shapes, so much larger than that of a buzzard, can often be seen soaring over the island, especially in the northern mountains and in the Lochranza area. Nesting sites are known, but are kept secret so as to protect the birds from the foolish antics of egg collectors and other crazed souvenir hunters. The crags on which they nest are often also used by ravens for the same purpose, and there are records of ravens stealing material from eagles' nests to help construct their own!

The red deer is the dominant animal of the moorlands and mountain corries, at least in the north of the island. A deer fence crosses the island from Brodick to Machrie, and is intended to pen the animals in the north so as to protect the forestry plantations and farmers' crops from their attentions. Stories of damage to some recently planted trees in the south of the island suggest that the fence, which looks so daunting when seen from the top of the String Road (NR 977359), may not be as effective as was hoped.

Presently deer numbers are large, recent surveys suggesting that more than 2,000 animals live in the north of the island. Arran was famed in Celtic legend for its deer, but over the centuries hunting for sport and for food and culling to protect crops reduced numbers greatly. By 1695, about 400 beasts were kept to provide sport for the Duke of Hamilton and his friends. Worries about the preservation of the stock were such that the local peasantry were penalised if they killed the deer, except in the case of an official cull. Despite this, by 1772 there were only a few tens of deer on the island. In 1859 fresh deer stock was imported from the mainland to revitalise the local bloodline, and numbers since then have risen to the present figure.

Although the largest numbers of deer are to be found in the high corries in summer, they are often to be seen grazing the slopes above the String Road (B880) and around the top of the Boguille, the road from Sannox to Lochranza. In this latter area, small herds can be seen sharing the fields with sheep around the farmhouse of Glen (NR 954502). Because deer will eat grass, heather, shoots on trees, turnips, seaweed, almost anything in fact, they are a major problem to the farmers in the north of the island, particularly in winter when conditions drive them down from the hills. The driver on the roads around Lochranza may need to hoot to clear a passage through the animals on occasion, and I know of at least one case where a car was damaged by a stag leaping over a fence and landing on the bonnet! So much for the shy retiring creatures of legend!

Two other creatures of mountain and moor deserve a brief mention. Wild mountain goats are no longer found on the island — though the name Goatfell suggests otherwise, it is likely that it is actually a corruption of the Gaelic for 'hill of the wind' — but a herd still survives on Holy Isle. Talk of letting the shooting rights on that island to parties of German hunters does not bode well for the future of these creatures, but at present nothing can be confirmed of any such arrangements.

Rather less attractive, but still an interesting feature of island wildlife, is the adder. In summer, adders can be found basking in the sun on rocks or on paths in several of the glens and moors. Despite its reputation it is a shy, inoffensive animal that would rather retire from view than attack passing tourists. That is not to say that it will not defend itself if annoyed by being poked with a stick or trodden on, but even if it does bite it is no more likely to be fatal than a wasp sting, except in the case of very young children. Records suggest that no one has died of an adder bite on Arran as far as is known, and it should be regarded as another part of that varied wildlife which supports the contention that the island is 'Scotland in miniature'.

CHAPTER 4

The Arrival of Man

There was no human life on Arran at the end of the glacial period, but as conditions improved and fish entered the rivers, animals and birds spread back over the land. So too Man slowly began to make an impact on the landscape. Initially the land would have been too poor to support any sort of agricultural settlement. There was, however, a rich harvest to be gleaned by the nomadic wanderer — berries, roots, fish and shellfish were all available to tempt the first 'tourists' to venture across to Arran.

The Mesolithic Visitors — Early Hunters

Although there is no direct evidence for the date of arrival of the first people to land in Arran after the ice ages, pollen analysis of sites near Lochranza and on Machrie Moor suggests that there may have been humans in the vicinity as long as 8,500 years ago. These first settlers would have crossed the seas from the west, from Northern Ireland, or possibly from Galloway, where evidence of such early settlement has long been known, but it is only relatively recently that traces of their presence have been discovered on Arran.

The initial visitors would have been small family groups, probably travelling by dugout canoes or skin boats. They were few in number, and pursued a nomadic way of life in which they basically followed the harvest, be it animal or vegetable. It appears that fishing and shellfish gathering in particular were the main sources of food. They probably lived in skin tents which they would take with them on their wanderings, so they left nothing in the way of permanent structures for future archaeologists to puzzle over. The main type of evidence for their presence is large mounds of shells, refuse from their shellfish collections, which have been found in various parts of western Scotland, but not on Arran. So how can we be sure that Arran was visited by these peoples?

To pursue their hunting and fishing activities, it is known that Mesolithic hunters created simple tools. Stone scrapers were used to prise limpets from rocks, while bone fish-hooks, harpoon heads, spear heads and scrapers aided the hunters of more mobile prey. It is these primitive tools, made of flint, quartz and pitchstone (a local rock found at Corriegills, near Brodick) which have been discovered on Arran, particularly at Auchareoch Farm (NR 995246) in the valley of Kilmory Water, and near Knockenkelly (NS 044274) by Whiting Bay, which prove that these early hunters roamed widely across the slowly afforesting semi-tundra landscapes of the island. A collection of such primitive tools, found on the island, can be seen in the Arran Heritage Museum at Brodick.

Because of their love of shellfish, these early people would have made their camp sites on or close to the beaches which would have been related to a slowly rising sea-level, possibly higher than at present. Thus some of the traces of their presence may have become buried under beach sands. They may also have looked at coastal caves such as King's Cave (NR 884310) as potential shelter, but given the higher sea-level of the time, it is possible that such caves would have been anything but dry places of refuge!

It is most unlikely that the Mesolithic inhabitants of Arran ever numbered more than a few tens of people, and when the next wave of settlement spread across to the island these pioneers would either have been driven out or, more likely, simply became integrated with the incomers.

The Next Wave — Neolithic Farmers

About 5,800 years ago, as the climate was becoming warmer and wetter as it rose towards the so-called 'Climatic Optimum', the first of the Neolithic or 'New Stone Age' settlers began to arrive in Arran. These people brought with them not only greatly improved stone tools but also the idea of permanent settlements based on agricultural practices. These ideas, which had originated in the Middle East at least a thousand years earlier, spread gradually throughout continental Europe to reach south-west Scotland and northern Ireland more or less simultaneously.

One of the stone circles on Machrie Moor. The stones, which stand up to 5 m in height, are only one of a whole series of prehistoric monuments to be found in the vicinity.

Neolithic tools differ from those of the Mesolithic in their range, style and quality of finish, being ground and polished rather than simply chipped into shape. The improved cutting edge that this gave allowed them to begin to tackle the task of cutting clearings in the forest, which was by this time firmly established over all but the highest parts of the island. The stone axe was a vital tool, for clearings in the forest were needed for both stock-rearing (cattle, sheep, goats and pigs) and crop-growing (wheat and barley). The areas with the best stone to make such axes were often quite remote from the sites to be cleared, and it seems that trade in axes and other tools took place all over the Firth of Clyde region. Certainly most of the axes found on Arran are not made from native rock and must have been brought with the first settlers or imported later.

Probably the greatest amount of information about Neolithic settlers in Arran relates not to the way they lived, but to what happened when they died. Associated with a more settled way of life came a much more elaborate ceremony of death, with tombs of various sorts and sizes, often containing not just a body or bodies, but also offerings such as tools and some quite elaborate pottery. The tombs followed a common pattern. They all contain a chamber constructed from large slabs of stone. Sometimes a row of such chambers was built at a site to form a 'gallery', each chamber being placed end-to-end with its neighbours. The body of the deceased would be placed in a chamber, which would then have been roofed with a rock slab. Once the burials of members of the group or family had filled all the chambers, stones were erected to mark the entrance, and then the entire structure was covered with a great cairn of boulders which could be two or three metres high.

Good examples of these chambered tombs can be seen at several places in Arran south of a line from Sannox (NS 015457) to Machrie (NR 891348), but they are absent from the more rugged lands of the north — possibly a reflection on less favourable conditions for agriculture in that area. Probably the largest of these tombs is at Carn Ban (NR 991262), a massive cairn in the forestry development area of southern Arran. It can be reached by taking the Forestry tracks to Auchareoch, either from Whiting Bay or from the A841 some 1,200 m east of Lagg.

There are too many sites of this type to describe in detail, but a good example, the chambered cairn at Torrylinn (NR 955211), can be reached easily by a path leading from the Post Office at Lagg towards the shore. The site is well preserved, and a plaque gives the visitor information as to what it is that he/she is seeing. The 'Giants' Graves' (NS 043247) near Whiting Bay are a rather less well-preserved series of chambered cairns, reached by a lung-bursting climb up a well-signposted path which branches from the Forestry path along Glen Ashdale. Other cairns can be seen at East Bennan (NR 994207), at Clauchog (NR 950212) and in the vicinity of the farm of Tormore (NR 903311).

A number of the cairns were raided by later settlers who used the stones for building, and on occasion made off with parts of the long-dead inhabitants as souvenirs! A dire tale is told of one such grave-robber who ventured to rifle the Torrylinn cairn, taking home one of the skulls it contained. From that day forth, severe winds shook his cottage even on the calmest of days and he became so frightened that he hastily reburied the bones, but all to no avail. He continued to be haunted until one day, as he was riding towards Lagg, he was thrown from his horse over an embankment and killed on the rocks below! The modern visitor would do well to heed this tale, though nowadays it would be the Ancient Monuments Commission of the Department of the Environment that would seek retribution.

The Bronze Age — the Monument Builders arrive

Some 4,100 years ago the first peoples familiar with the working of metals came to Britain. They were rather different from the Neolithic people whom they supplanted, being rather taller and with a rounder head. These invaders landed first on the North Sea coasts of Britain, and spread slowly across the land from there. To judge by types of pottery and other objects discovered by archaeologists, the people who arrived in Arran at this time seem to have belonged to a 'western' strain who migrated northwards along the Irish Sea coastlines and into the west coast of Scotland, bringing with them both a new way of life and a wider and better range of tools and materials.

The Bronze Age culture was more highly organised and social than the Neolithic had been. They continued and extended agriculture, being able to penetrate into denser forests than before because of their superior tools. With the establishment of more permanent settlement patterns, a class system began to evolve, ruled by a warrior aristocracy, to judge from finds of gold weapons and ornaments. They also had knowledge of rudimentary engineering and science techniques which they used in the erection of the standing stones which form the most striking memorials to the former existence of these people. If, as some suspect, stones were erected in circles for purposes of astronomical observation and prediction, then the warriors may have shared their position of influence with a scientific or religious élite.

It seems that significant trade routes in copper and tin developed at this time. Tin was brought mainly from Cornwall, while a major source of copper was the area around Kilmartin, in mid-Argyll. It is known that extensive trade took place along routeways stretching from north-east Scotland through the Great Glen to Argyll, and then down through the Firth of

Clyde to the Irish Sea and on to the tin deposits of the West
Country of England. Arran was in an ideal location to take
advantage of these lines of trade, and it is hardly surprising
that the island is rich in relics of this time.

The techniques for smelting and then casting bronze from
the raw ores would have given those who had the skill a rare
degree of power in that early society, and some of the
ornaments and weapons that have been found on the island are
of a beauty and workmanship that could be afforded by only
the wealthiest of people, even today. The fact that such objects
are usually found in burial cists accompanying their owners to
the next world indicates the importance which was attached to
them.

A bronze dagger with gold fillet, recovered from a cist in a
massive burial cairn (now largely demolished) at Cairn Farm,
near Blackwaterfoot (NR 898282), is of a style associated with
the Wessex culture of south-west England (the builders of
Stonehenge). This cultural link is further emphasised by the
style of fragments of jet necklaces found in chambers in cairns
near Lamlash (at Dunan Beag — NS 026330) and near
Tormore Farm near Blackwaterfoot (NR 894324) where the
chamber is actually built into the wall of a byre.

The presence of these 'Wessex-style' goods has been used to
suggest that in the early Bronze Age at least, the inhabitants of
Arran may have been a flint-using group under the control of
overlords from Wessex who wished to safeguard the trade-
routes bringing the precious copper ore from Argyll. Some
may see a parallel here to the present-day relationship between
the Scots and the English!

The form of burial was to change somewhat during the
course of the Bronze Age. At the beginning, burial was in
simple cists, sometimes in passages driven into Neolithic cairns,
sometimes with a cairn and sometimes with no surface marking
at all. The body would be fitted into this small space in a
crouched position, and with it an earthenware pot, presumably
containing food for the journey to the hereafter, and whatever
other treasures the deceased had wished to keep. Such cists
have been found in several places, most commonly in the
Machrie, Shiskine and Brodick areas. One such example,
found in the old deer park at Brodick Castle, has been

Ancient traditions such as Hallowe'en are still widely celebrated on Arran. Here a group of guisers set off around Lamlash to perform party pieces at houses, in return for which they will receive small gifts of money or fruit.

transported to the Heritage Museum at Brodick and reassembled there for public inspection.

Burials were of a different form again by the middle Bronze Age (about 3,700 years ago). Now cremation was the norm, with the charred bones being placed in a funerary urn which was then buried. Such urns have been found on Arran, but appear to contain no gold or bronze objects of value. However, some beautiful gold armlets and other ornaments of this period have been discovered on Arran, most notably at Ormidale in Brodick, at Kiscadale by Whiting Bay, and at Whitefarland (NR 865423) where a lock-ring and a dress fastener were found under a boulder near the road. These were of an Irish style of design, and are probably late Bronze Age in origin (3,200 – 2,200 years old).

The picture of Bronze Age life in Arran is not just confined to burial sites. We know from the finding of fossil cereal grains that agriculture was practised in the Machrie area of the island as much as 5,300 years ago. We also know that the climate

during the Bronze Age was deteriorating, becoming cooler and
less hospitable, although pollen analysis confirms that restricted
agriculture continued through that period. But it was not a
time to live in caves or skin tents, for farming required more
permanent dwellings.

In areas like Machrie Moor, low circular ridges or banks,
often picked out by heather, contrasting with the grasses of the
boggy interior of the circle, have been identified in great
numbers. These so-called 'hut circles' are the foundations of
dwellings, circular houses eight to twelve metres in diameter,
which were probably roofed in thatch. They were long thought
to have been built in the Iron Age, but recent work indicates
some are Bronze Age. Low banks of stones outside these hut
circles mark the edges of small fields which would have been
tilled using primitive ploughs. Hut circles are difficult to locate
on the ground, but quite a good one is to be found just north
of the path to the Machrie Moor stone circles at a point where
it starts to climb towards the moor (NR 903326). Another well-
defined set can be seen in the moorland near Kilpatrick
(NR 905266). From the air, they can easily be picked out by the
patterns of vegetation.

The Bronze Age is the period associated with the feature
most people think of when asked to name a prehistoric site —
Stonehenge. Arran too has its share of standing stones and
stone circles. Again these are largely confined to the southern
part of the island, being most common around Machrie,
though excellent examples are found at many places in the
'lowland' part of Arran.

Standing stones are so common that even the least energetic
visitors to Arran will have seen examples of them — probably
without realising their significance. The sandstone slab that
stands about two metres high beside the A841 opposite the
north-east corner of the playground at Brodick school is a good
example, as is the monument that rises some three metres
above the grazing sheep in a field on the left of the minor road
leading to Auchencar Farm (NR 891364) and the 'Sheepskin
Shop'. These solitary stones are usually slabs cut from rocks
such as sandstone which can be split easily along cracks and
joints, probably by the use of levers and wedges. How such
slabs were moved into position is not known, but ropes, rollers,
sledges and sheer brute manpower are the most likely tools.

The impact of the individual standing stone on the senses is quite substantial, but the effect is much greater when the stone is merely one of a group forming a circle. Probably the finest single circle in Arran is at Auchagallon (NR 893346) which is signposted up a farm track more or less opposite the telephone call box in Machrie. This is a large circle of slabs which is said to have had a cist within it. In common with most of the major Arran stone circles, it has a splendid view, and it has been suggested that most stone circles were erected so as to be visible from afar. This has added strength to the idea that they had some sort of religious or ceremonial function.

Some stone circles have been built using rounded boulders rather than massive sandstone slabs. The boulders, mostly of granite, were carried from the northern hills by glacier ice which, upon melting, dropped them in locations all over the southern part of the island. The inhabitants therefore had a supply of material with which to build monuments even when they lived far from a source of the large sandstone slabs. Good examples of these boulder-based circles can be seen just to the east of the summit of the A841 Brodick to Lamlash road (NS 018336), where an incomplete ring of boulders just peeps above the heather. This location commands the most magnificent view of the northern mountains, slightly curtailed by recent forest growth.

If the visitor has only the time or inclination to visit a single site to see stone circles and standing stones, then he/she should be directed to Machrie Moor. Here, in an area in the centre of a lowland overlooked by rolling uplands with the northern granite peaks keeping a distant presence, is one of the most remarkable concentrations of archaeological sites in Scotland. Here are stone circles, hut circles, burial cists and other features, the full extent of which is gradually being revealed by an ongoing programme of excavation.

The way to the stones is signposted from the A841 at a point (NR 895331) where a few vehicles can be parked just off the main road. A farm track, unsuitable for cars, leads from here out onto the moorland, passing on the way some rather small standing stones and stone circles, as well as hut circles. The first of the major monuments (NR 909324) is composed of two almost complete circles of granite boulders, one inside the other. In one of the stones there is a hole near one of the edges. According to later Celtic legend, this hole was where the great hero Fingal used to tie his dog. From this site, looking to the east, the eye is drawn by the most dramatic prehistoric monuments on Arran. Rising out the moor to a height of three to four metres are four major slabs of sandstone (NR 911324). On closer inspection, one of these weathered slabs is seen to be standing apart from the other three, and is now thought to be the last remnant of a circle of nine such stones. The other three are part of another circle, at the centre of which a cist was found.

The impact of these stones on the imagination, particularly if the weather is misty and the eye is not drawn to the surrounding hills, can be very strong indeed. A sense of mystery and of communication with the past, can grip the onlooker in much the same way that the first glimpse of the interior of one of the great mediaeval cathedrals can do. Who is to say that these structures did not serve a similar function to a cathedral as far as their builders were concerned? Despite a great deal of conjecture and the imaginative outpourings of many fertile minds, we still do not know the exact use to which these enigmatic structures, these sentinels from the past, were put. The mystery is part of their attraction.

The Iron Age — the Coming of the Celts

As the Bronze Age drew to a close, a new wave of invasion affected the British Isles. Celtic-speaking tribes spread out from Central Europe and invaded Britain from the south and west, gradually spreading northwards, ultimately to reach the Shetland Islands. There is still some dispute about whether or not this was a mass invasion or simply a gradual infiltration over a lengthy period as a result of trading. There is no doubt that from about 2,400 years ago the use of iron for the making of tools began to be adopted in Britain. This may have been a result of direct trading with Celtic incomers, or by the original inhabitants copying techniques of smelting from these people.

One aspect of the Iron Age which gave rise to the idea of large-scale invasion by Celtic hordes is the number of forts and other defensive structures that have been identified and associated with the period. These gave rise to the idea that this

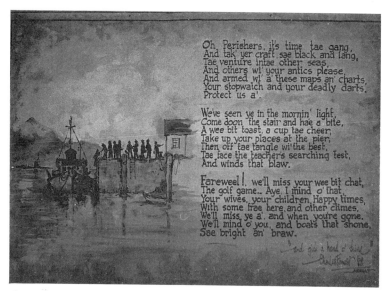

Oh, Perishers, it's time tae gang,
And tak' yer craft sae black an' lang,
Tae venture intae other seas,
And others wi' your antics please,
And armed wi' a' these maps an' charts,
Your stopwatch and your deadly darts,
Protect us a'.

We've seen ye in the mornin' light,
Come doon the stair and hae a bite,
A wee bit toast, a cup tae cheer,
Take up your places at the pier,
Then off tae tangle wi' the best,
Tae face the teacher's searching test,
And winds that blaw.

Fareweel!, we'll miss your wee bit chat,
The golf game.. Aye, I mind o' that,
Your wives, your children, Happy times,
With some free here and other climes,
We'll miss ye a'. and when you're gone,
We'll mind o' you, and boats that shone,
See bright an' braw.

Over the years, Arran has had many connections with the 'Perishers' undergoing a submariners' training course in the Firth of Clyde. During the course, many of the trainee officers have been billeted in the Douglas Hotel in Brodick and have been so active socially that a bar in the hotel has been called the 'Perishers' Bar'. This illuminated manuscript, illustrating the bond that grew up over time between the locals and the sailors, was produced on the island when it was announced that the courses were to end.

was a time of intense conflict, almost permanent warfare between tribal groups. Certainly it is known that Celtic chieftains fought for the 'fun' of it, and indulged in cattle rustling and (presumably) the rape, pillage and murder that are presumed to be the prerogative of the later Viking adventurers!

One problem which has hampered our understanding of the Iron Age way of life is the fact that, unlike bronze, iron rusts. Thus we have far fewer artifacts from this time with which to reconstruct the past, and the main evidence comes from fortified buildings such as brochs and duns. The sites chosen for such structures were usually on hilltops or other easily defended positions. Some were quite small, possibly family-sized; others, such as the massive fort at Drumadoon (NR 886293), may have been a tribal centre into which the local population retreated, together with their cattle, at the first sign of a raid. The site covers about twelve acres and is protected to the west by vertical cliffs and elsewhere by a stone wall some three metres thick. It must have been a daunting prospect for any would-be invader to contemplate scaling those defences, and it is little wonder that the area is believed to have been a centre of population at that time.

The usual construction of a fort was for an outer ditch to be dug, inside which a wall of stones, earth and timbers would be erected. Some of these forts have been vitrified, that is, burnt at such a high temperature that the stone melted and flowed to form a solid cinder-like material. It is not known whether this was done deliberately as a method of strengthening the fort, or, more likely, as a result of the fort being destroyed by burning after capture or even by accident. There is one example of such a fort on Arran. It is built on a clifftop just to the north of Sannox Bay (NS 017461), but is difficult to see clearly, partly because it consists of low mounds of vitrified blocks rather than a major rampart, and partly because the site is now covered with woodland which obscures many of the remains.

Other types of fort include the broch and the dun, basically variants on the theme of a small circular dry-stone walled fort. The term 'broch' is usually given to the compact, high-walled structures of the north of Scotland, while 'dun' is the term used for small forts in the west of the country.

In Arran the remains can be seen of no fewer than fifteen Iron Age forts. They are located in all parts of the island except the west coast between Drumadoon and Lochranza, and are all found on hilltops, natural promontories or cliff tops. It is not likely that these forts were all in use simultaneously, but rather that they were built one at a time over a period of many years. Possibly new ones were constructed every time an older one was destroyed or burnt down. The span of time over which this process continued is reflected in the different styles in which they were constructed.

The large enclosed hilltop at Drumadoon has already been described, but a similar one in an even better vantage point can be seen in the form of a series of ditches running around the top of the hill called Cnoc Ballygown (NR 920292). This must have been a very exposed site a long way from arable land, and, as Horace Fairhurst says in his excellent book, *Exploring*

Arran's Past, it is tempting to think that this remote and very bleak fort was later supplanted by the more accessible structure at Drumadoon.

A similar sort of high remote site is occupied by the fort on the hill above Lochranza (NR 927503), while even higher is the fort known as Torr an t-Sean Chaisteal (NS 002474) overlooking North Glen Sannox and the Arran mountains. This fort is better preserved than many others, possibly because of its remoteness, and the lines of the walls can still be seen quite clearly by the visitor stalwart enough to clamber up the heathery slopes to inspect it.

Smaller forts of the dun type have been found in the southern part of the island. One which can be seen from the road is Torr a Chaisteal (NR 922233) at Corriecravie, located on top of a small hillock overlooking the raised beach platform. More spectacular still is Dun Fionn (NS 047339), a small enclosure marked by a low bank around the top of a cliff near the highest point of the path from Corriegills (reached by taking the signposted branch from the Brodick to Lamlash road) to Lamlash via Clauchlands Point. Although small, the attraction of Dun Fionn is the site, perched on the very edge of a 150-m high cliff overlooking the sea and commanding spectacular views over the Firth of Clyde and the northern hills.

Dun Fionn also overlooks the northern entrance to the magnificent harbour at Lamlash. The southern entrance too is guarded by an Iron Age fort, at King's Cross (NS 056283). This fort, situated right beside the remains of a Second World War gun emplacement and a Viking burial site, is a small stone-built dun about eleven metres in diameter. The walls are now only about one metre high at most, partly overgrown with brambles and whins, and could be missed quite easily even though a coastal path goes right through the centre of the structure. The site repays the effort of finding it though, for in the quiet still of a summers evening it is possible to sit on the rampart and gaze out to the slopes of Holy Isle, looking much as the Iron Age builders must have seen it, and again feel the link between the past and present in Arran. At such a moment, the spirit of those heroic times can still reach out over the ages to touch the modern soul.

CHAPTER 5

Monks, Norsemen and Normans

We now enter a period of Arran's story from which very little in the way of structures, buildings or burial sites has been preserved. It is also a period in which the first detailed records of history begin to introduce individual characters in more or less precisely dated situations into the Arran story. Throughout the period in question (over a thousand years) the constant theme is Arran as a frontier area, constantly passing from Highland to Lowland influence and back again. In some ways, the island can be said to have aspects of the whole of Scottish history in its own story, though only within certain limits.

The Coming of Christianity to Arran

Towards the close of the Iron Age, Arran was inhabited by a Pictish tribe, probably the same people who built the duns described in the previous chapter. On various bases of evidence, these people have been linked with the northern group of Picts, even though they left no history of their activities on Arran – not even placenames. Their tenancy of the island spans the gap between prehistory and history, living as they did during the well-documented years of the Roman presence in Scotland.

The Romans appear to have passed Arran by, although the possible remains of a Roman harbour have been reported from Irvine. Perhaps they simply regarded Arran as a dark and mysterious place not worth invading, particularly when they were having so much trouble holding on to their mainland territories anyway!

Spreading originally from Ireland into Argyll and offshore islands, the Scots, a Gaelic-speaking tribe, pushed the Picts out of the district and established the kingdom of Dalriada in the region, possibly in the second or third century AD. This was originally part of a Dalriadan kingdom based in northern Ireland, but by AD 575 it was agreed that there should be a

Holy Isle, seen from the tourist and fishing village of Whiting Bay.

separate kingdom, also called Dalriada, in Scotland. The echoes of this decision were to be heard down the years in varying degrees until the sixteenth century, for the territory of Dalriada was later to become a major power base in Scottish history.

Links with the early Christian church were to become well established in Dalriada, especially in Argyll and around the Firth of Clyde. Several holy men are known to have set out from Ulster to found monasteries or to become hermits for a while in the fastnesses of Dalriada. The presence of these bearers of the Christian flame in the region has been marked by a number of place names, especially 'Kil-' as in Kildonan and Kilbride, indicating the existence of a 'cill' or monk's cell at that location. Physical remnants such as buildings dating from this time are rare indeed, though caves such as St. Molaise's Cell on Holy Isle and King's Caves on the west coast of Arran have been linked by tradition and some historical fact to these early Christian voyagers.

Where the first monks to visit Arran came from is a matter of some conjecture. One view is that the Christian influence in the area may have spread south from Iona, where St. Columba had founded his monastery by AD 563, rather than directly

from Ireland or the Galloway area where St. Ninian had
founded a mission as early as AD 397. It would certainly be
surprising if the Gallovidian monks had not been tempted to
visit the mountainous island in the Firth of Clyde that can
clearly be seen from many parts of their domain.

Legend has it that the Irish monk St. Brendan made a
voyage in AD 545, during which he visited the Western Isles.
The present inhabitants of Bute are known as Brandanes, after
the Saint, who is thought to have visited their island. If it is true
that he came to Bute on his travels, then St. Brendan must
have sailed right by Arran, although no legends exist to suggest
that he actually visited the island. What is certain is that by
AD 574 St. Blane had arrived in Bute, possibly from Iona.
Arran would thus appear to be at the border between areas
which were Christianised directly from Ireland, and those
which fell within the orbit of Iona.

The holy man most associated with Arran is St. Molaise, who
was born in Argyllshire, educated largely in Ireland, and who
eventually came to Arran to live the life of a hermit in a shallow
cave on Holy Isle. The date of his arrival is not known with any
degree of precision. The *Book of Arran* puts it at AD 680 but
Robert MacLellan will say no more than that it was after
AD 580. However, he thinks that St. Molaise died in AD 639 in
Ireland, a date which is incompatible with his supposed landing
in AD 680! St. Molaise gave his name to Lamlash (a corruption
of the Gaelic for 'island of Molaise'), and was the critical factor
in the naming of Holy Isle. The cave (NS 060295) in which he
lived is really no more than a shallow indentation beneath an
overhanging rock slab, fronted by a low masonry wall and
entered from ground level by a small flight of steps. The *Book
of Arran* suggests that in part at least the wall may have been
built up until it met the overhanging rock, thus protecting the
Saint from the worst of the elements. A number of carvings
exist on the overhanging rock wall of the cave, but most are
later grafitti, including a set of Viking runes which may date
from 1263, at the time of the Battle of Largs.

Not far from the monk's cell on Holy Isle there is a spring
known as St. Molaise's Well, the waters from which were much
in demand for curative purposes. These holy associations led to
a monastery being founded on the island. This structure,
reputed to date from the beginning of the thirteenth century,

was situated close by the site of the present pier (NS 052308), but no trace remains at present of it or of the associated burial ground, which until the end of the eighteenth century was the principal graveyard on Arran.

At one time Holy Isle was a major centre of pilgrimage. This is a little difficult at present, as the current owners (most recent in a series of rather brief ownerships) are trying to sell the island for over £1 million (possibly in the form of burial plots of 'Holy' ground to North Americans). As an alternative, they are also reported (1988) to be investigating the possibility of bottling and selling water from St. Molaise's Well. Either way, the casual visitor nowadays is discouraged from coming to the island. The small open ferry that used to take visitors on day trips to the island from Lamlash has not been able to ply its trade for the past few years, and the island is now almost as much of a refuge as it was during St. Molaise's tenancy.

Apart from the 'Kil-' placenames already mentioned, which are common in the south of the island, more concrete evidence that St. Molaise may not have been the only Christian in the area comes from Kildonan. Here, records suggest that a number of early Christian burials have been found near Kildonan farmhouse (NS 035212), associated with what may have been the remains of a chapel. Further west at Kilpatrick (NR 905266) there are a series of remains of a cashel and an associated round building. This site, reached by following the signs to 'Kilpatrick Dun' from the main road about a mile south of Blackwaterfoot, was interpreted in the *Book of Arran* as an early monastic site, possibly associated with St. Brendan, but more recent knowledge makes that interpretation rather doubtful. It is not known at present just what the true origin of the site is, but a visit is worthwhile both for the site itself and for the splendid views it affords over the Shiskine lowlands, Kilbrannan Sound and Kintyre, and on to Ireland.

The Norse Interlude

Into the relatively peaceful environment of eighth-century Dalriada, with its well-established political structure and a slowly expanding Christian religion, came a new and sometimes violent force which was to produce a permanent change in the region. The Vikings, sailing from Norway and

Denmark, came initially in search of booty and slaves, but later to settle, trade and impose their sovereignty on the land. In Dalriada, the first raids of which we have knowledge affected Iona (AD 794) and Kintyre (AD 797). Arran is unlikely to have escaped these raids for very much longer. A site at the mouth of the Blairmore Burn (NS 033319), now occupied by Douglas Villa, revealed on excavation a mound of skulls and a sword of early Viking type. This may mark the site of a battle of some description, possibly a raid by the Norsemen on the inhabitants of the area.

A slightly more substantial relic of the Viking presence in Arran can be seen at King's Cross, where, next to the Iron Age dun (NS 056283), is an elongated mound, partly overgrown and partly destroyed by the wear of feet, as a footpath runs right along the length of the feature. From this mound were recovered some metal rivets, charcoal and burnt bone fragments and a coin minted in York about AD 850. The mound is interpreted as a cremation burial in a boat, presumably of an important person. The event must postdate the coin, but the exact date is not known, nor is it sure just how a coin from York came to Arran.

As Viking settlement and trading became better established, so their political influence strengthened. By the end of the eleventh century, Magnus Barefoot had established the Isles and Kintyre as part of the Norwegian kingdom, though in effect it would have seen a Viking presence for a couple of centuries before that. At the end of the ninth century. Vikings attacked the kingdom of Alba (mainland Scotland), laying siege to Dumbarton and fighting other battles on the mainland. The easiest route for their fleets to follow would have included the waters of the Firth of Clyde, and it is likely that the Arranachs of the time would have seen the sails of Norse fleets moving over the waters of the Firth of Clyde on many occasions.

Although there are few relics from the Viking period in Arran, placenames of that time give some clue as to the lot of the common man. Norse names do occur in Arran, for example Brodick (Breidvik = broad bay), Sannox (Sandvik = sandy bay), Goat Fell (possibly), Ormidale, Chalmadale, Scorrodale, but the majority of placenames are Gaelic. Several of these are associated with rents for land, for example

Brodick Castle looms above the village golf course as its turrets rise above the trees which grow so luxuriantly in the policies.

Penrioch, Dippen and Benlister, which all relate to pence, a unit of currency introduced by the Vikings. In addition, the old Gaelic 'Achadh', meaning a field worked as a communal open-field system, crops up in modern names like Auchencairn and Auchenhew. Yet the Vikings themselves had a system of individual land ownership. These contradictions are explained if we imagine a limited Viking presence, acting as overlords to a native Scots population who paid them rent for the lands that they worked. Thus, from being bringers only of death and destruction, over the centuries the Vikings were to establish a more peaceful relationship with the natives of Arran.

The Rise of the Gall-Gaels and the Fall of the Norse

In the Isles, as might be expected, the Viking overlords seem to have been unable or unwilling to isolate themselves from the charms of the native Scots maidens. The mixed-race offspring of these relationships were known as Gall-Gaels, literally 'foreign Gaels' or 'stranger Gaels', who were brought up Gaelic-speaking but who occupied positions of power and influence within the land. Chafing at Norse sovereignty, they began a struggle to create an independent kingdom in the Isles, free of the influence of both the Norwegian and Scottish kingdoms,

61

the latter of which was now a real nation under the rule of Malcolm Canmore.

The first Gall-Gael to emerge from the mists of history as a clear leader of his people was Somerled, who in a sea battle in 1156 established himself as the ruler of what was virtually an independent domain, but one which acknowledged Norse overlordship of the islands and Scottish overlordship of the mainland territories. It is known that galleys from Arran were available on a mercenary basis at that time, and it is likely that the island contributed men and boats to Somerled's fleet.

Following his death on an expedition to the upper Clyde estuary, two of Somerled's nephews are known to have fought over the title of 'King' of the Isles. From Ranald, the triumphant one, sprang the line of the MacDonalds of the Isles, and from his father, Dugall, came the MacDougalls and the Campbells, names which are still very common in Argyll and parts of the Hebrides.

Although the territory of the Isles continued to exist for over a century, it came under increasing pressure from the Scottish throne. Alexander II of Scotland (1214-47) asserted his authority over mainland Argyll, thereby isolating the Clyde islands from the rest of the territories of the Isles. The waters of the Clyde had now become a frontier zone of political and military intrigue. Alexander, High Steward of Scotland, had married a descendant of Somerled, and through this link claimed ownership of the Clyde islands, bringing them under nominal Scots control. This, together with the loss of Kintyre, led Ospak, a descendent of Somerled, to appeal to Norway for help, indicating that he preferred Norse overlordship to Scottish rule. He returned with a Norwegian fleet, attacked Rothesay Castle and raided Kintyre, but could make no permanent impression on Scottish control of the Clyde, and eventually returned to Norway. Alexander II of Scotland then offered to buy the islands from Norway, but was refused. Although intending then to take them by force, he died before he was able to embark on this course.

It was to fall to Alexander III to complete the task of lifting the Norwegian yoke from the islands. The pressures he put on the Isles alarmed King Hakon of Norway to such an extent that he scoured his kingdom for men to form a great fleet which came to Scotland, eventually anchoring in the huge natural harbour of Lamlash Bay. The galleys stayed in the bay beneath the sheltering bulk of Holy Isle for many days while negotiations with Alexander of Scotland started. It was probably at this juncture that most of the runes found in St. Molaise's Cell were carved, including one which translates as 'Vigleikr the king's marshal cut this'.

The negotiations dragged on, Alexander being willing to concede joint overlordship of the Clyde islands, but Hakon not being agreeable to this. At length the fleet moved to Cumbrae, and the talks continued until the Norwegians lost patience and started to harry some of the Clyde coasts. On 1 October 1263, a storm stranded some of the Viking fleet on the mainland at Largs. These ships were attacked by the Scots, the Norwegians sent reinforcements, and the battle proper commenced, lasting for a whole day, at the end of which the Norse abandoned their hopes of defeating the Scots, and retreated to Lamlash again, a much less imposing sight than they had been less than a month earlier. From there, Hakon left to return to Norway, having given (or so he imagined) Arran to one Margad, another of the line of Somerled. This was a hollow gift, for Hakon died in Kirkwall on the return journey, and his successor agreed in 1266 to sell the Isles to Scotland. Thus five hundred years of Norse influence, marked in Arran by no more than a few placenames and a couple of archaeological sites, came to an end. The main Norse legacy is in the Gall-Gael bloodstock, which is still strong in these areas, and can be seen in the colouring and stature of many of the inhabitants.

Feudal Arran and the Normans

Norman influence came to Scotland, and Arran, long after their invasion of England in 1066. They were initially welcomed as warrior knights who were willing to serve the Crown in return for the grant of lands for themselves. The feudal system was introduced during the reign of David I (1124-53), bringing with it a totally new form of land ownership as far as the natives of Scotland were concerned. Instead of land being a communal or tribal property, it was appropriated by the Crown, given to men, usually of Norman ancestry, who had nothing in common with the native peoples, who themselves then handed out smaller portions of it to their chosen subordinates. These new overlords often did not even speak the same language as the natives, who were forced to live as serfs to their masters. With the feudal system also came the law of direct succession of property, an alien concept to the Gaelic speakers who traditionally decided succession using the law of tanistry, by which new leaders were elected by tribal groupings each time a chief or king died. This was the principle under which the ancestors of Somerled had operated, and his descendants were to continue to try and regain power and land on Arran until at least the middle of the fifteenth century.

The typical Norman approach to newly granted land was to build a castle on it and then use the land for hunting, and the peasantry were forced to work and pay taxes to support their new overlord. In the islands, the Norman barons sometimes strengthened their claim to the land by marrying into Gall-Gael families of power. For example, in the late twelfth century Alexander, the High Steward of Scotland and founder of what was to become the royal house of Stewart, a Norman, laid his claim to Arran and Bute on the basis of marriage to a great-granddaughter of Somerled. Once Arran had been sold by the Norwegians to the Scottish Crown in 1266, then its effective overlords henceforth were Normans.

The usual early Norman castle followed the style known as 'motte and bailey', the motte being a large artificial mound, on the top of which was a wooden fortification, while outside this lay the bailey, an area where the retainers, servants etc. lived. Later the wooden structure evolved into the more permanent stone castle, but at least the motte usually survived to indicate the former presence of such a stronghold to the archaeologist. No such motte has been found in Arran, though the most likely site for one is at Brodick Castle. The oldest part of the present building is late thirteenth century, but it is known that an earlier fortification stood at that site and featured in the saga of Robert the Bruce and Arran.

Edward I of England first subjugated Scotland in the wake of a dispute over the succession to the Scottish throne. Edward chose John Balliol from three contenders, one of whom was the grandfather of Robert the Bruce. Balliol was crowned in 1292, but when he concluded a treaty with the French in 1296, Edward used this as an excuse to bring an army north, which led to the Wars of Independence (1296-1320). Edward granted Arran to one Thomas Bysset, a Norman, whose ancestor, Walter Bysset, had been killed on the island in 1251, presumably in one of the skirmishes between the Scottish nobles and the descendants of Somerled.

By 1306 a fleet, under the control of Hugh Bysset, together with the Stewart descendant John of Menteith, was sailing the waters of the Clyde on behalf of Edward, with the particular mission to stamp out the followers of Robert the Bruce in the isles. Bruce, the grandson of one of the unsuccessful competitors for the Scottish throne in 1292, had himself crowned King of Scotland in 1306, for which act he had eventually to flee to Rathlin Island, off the Ulster coast. There he stayed until the spring of 1307, when he returned to Scotland and began the campaign which was to lead to the Declaration of Arbroath (1320) and an independent Scottish nation.

Arran was to play a significant part in this story of the return of the Bruce to eventual triumph. Two of his principal lieutenants, Douglas and Boyd, sailed before the main fleet with instructions to land on Arran and harry the garrison there. This garrison, under the command of John Hastings, another of the three competitors for the Scottish Crown in 1292, who had now been granted the earldom of Menteith by Edward I, was based at Brodick Castle. This was presumably the same site as the present castle occupies, though no trace of this early structure remains. Douglas and Boyd landed on the west coast, probably at either Machrie or Blackwaterfoot, and then crossed the island to Brodick. There they ambushed and captured some supply boats bringing provisions for the castle, killing virtually all of the men unloading them. Some soldiers from the castle came to help their comrades but were chased back into the fortress. After this, Douglas, Boyd and their party retreated to some sort of stronghold in a 'woddy glen'. This is thought to be Glen Cloy, where the old structure commonly called 'Bruce's Castle' is situated (NR 992339). In all probability this is an Iron Age dun, and the adventurers were simply taking advantage of a relic of Arran's past for their own purposes.

Robert the Bruce followed Douglas and Boyd to Arran within a few days, his total force being thirty-three small galleys and about 300 men. He landed on the east coast of the island, probably in Whiting Bay or possibly Lamlash Bay, and found quarters in a clachan or 'fermtoun' in the area. The locals, who appear to have been solidly behind Bruce despite his Norman ancestry, led him to where Douglas and Boyd were, and the united group returned to their headquarters. The most likely location for their base lies somewhere around King's Cross (NS 050280). From here the Bruce would have been able to see the fire at Turnberry in Ayrshire which signalled him to cross to the mainland and begin the campaign which led eventually to his triumph over the English.

The King's Caves (NR 884309) on the west coast are popularly thought to be the place where Bruce waited for the beckoning beacon to be lit on the mainland, and some even place the famous episode with the spider there. There is no evidence to support either of these stories, especially as the Ayrshire coast cannot be seen from this area! However, it may have served as a shelter during his earlier flight to Rathlin in 1306, or may possibly have been linked with the Douglas and Boyd 'expedition' to Arran, as they are known to have first landed not far away.

Bruce's affection for the people of Arran was demonstrated by his forming a personal bodyguard, known as the Brandani, from the men of Bute and Arran. Some Arran families are reputed to have obtained their lands by charter from the Bruce. Certainly land grants were made to the Fullartons of Glencloy by Robert II, grandson of the Bruce, sometime before 1371. By the end of the century the Fullartons had also gained title to areas around Brodick Bay and to part of the south end of the island near Kildonan.

Prior to this, the island had been for a while the property of the Menteiths who, far from being persecuted for their earlier support of Edward I, had regained favour by marriage into Bruce's family. For a time they occupied the strategic castle of Lochranza (NR 933507), built on a narrow spit guarding the

Fierce storms lashed the island in February 1989, virtually destroying the old pier at Lochranza and almost washing Lochranza Castle into the sea. In this view, taken at the height of the hurricane, the castle appears almost to be floating in the waves. Fortunately the damage to the building was relatively slight, though the access road was ripped up by the force of the breakers.

entrance to the bay. Little is known of the precise history of the castle, but it was a stronghold of the Menteith family during the fourteenth century, and was referred to by Fordum in AD 1400 as a 'royal' castle believed to have been a base for hunting trips by kings and their retinues. The castle was passed in 1452 to the Montgomeries by James II, who hoped that by granting them much of the north-west of the island, they would secure this corner against the ravages of the Lords of the Isles, descendants of Somerled, who were still trying to lay claim to Arran.

These were turbulent times on Arran. At the end of the fourteenth century, apart from the Fullartons and the Menteiths, the Sheriff of Bute, a Stewart, also had lands on the island. In 1406 Robert III granted Kildonan Castle and some lands in south-east Arran to yet another Stewart, a bastard son of his. This is virtually the only mention in history of Kildonan Castle (NS 037210), the ruined keep which stands atop a low cliff looking out to the island of Pladda and the southern approaches to Arran. The castle, about which little is known, is now in a very poor state of repair and is dangerous even to approach closely.

In the same year as Robert III granted the lands of Kildonan (1406), Brodick Castle was burned down by an English fleet which had been sent to lay waste to the lands around the Clyde as part of the recriminations for breaches of a recently signed truce between England and Scotland. Not long after, yet more problems began to arise with the descendants of Somerled. These came to a head with the dispatch of a fleet of 70 galleys by the Lord of the Isles to harry the Ayrshire coast. This force then turned its attention to Arran, capturing and destroying the recently rebuilt Brodick Castle in 1455. This proved to be the climax of a long period of raids on Arran by men of Kintyre and Knapdale, all of which involved much slaughter, loss of crops and livestock and laying waste of farmland. Arran was suffering a lot at this time for its position on the outer fringes of the lands controlled by the kings of Scotland.

In 1467 Sir Thomas Boyd (descendant of the man who was with Bruce and Douglas on Arran) was created Earl of Arran and granted the royal lands on the island by James III. Boyd soon fell into disgrace and his title and lands became forfeit to the Crown. In 1503, one James Hamilton (of yet another Norman family) was made Earl of Arran in his stead. Thus began a family association with the island which has lasted until modern times.

At this time, apart from all the lands held by the Fullartons, the Montgomeries and the Hamiltons on Arran, the Stewarts of Bute now had title to all the lands between Corriegills and Kildonan. Feuds between the Hamiltons and the Stewarts continued the tradition of local strife on the island, and led to a raid by two sons of the Sheriff of Bute on the island, in the course of which Brodick Castle was 'destroyed'. The castle seems to have been rebuilt quickly enough thereafter, for in 1544 an English force under the Earl of Lennox was to destroy it yet again.

The Hamilton family had the opportunity to extend their grip over Arran during the regency of Mary, Queen of Scots. Hamilton was appointed regent, and took advantage of this to force the Stewarts to sell all their lands on the island except for Corriegills. In the years which followed, Hamilton power was to increase still further, though with some waverings. In 1599, one of the Hamilton family was in such good favour with James VI that he was created 1st Marquis of Hamilton.

The Wars of the Covenants did not entirely pass Arran by. The Hamiltons were Royalists, while the Campbells of Kintyre were supporters of the Covenant. These latter used this as an excuse to renew the ancient disputes over Arran. The Campbells seized Brodick Castle in 1639 and again in 1646, laying waste to much of the island in the process.

During the English Civil War the Hamiltons fought on the side of Charles I, while the 2nd Duke received a fatal injury at the Battle of Worcester (1652) when fighting in support of Charles II. A Cromwellian force was dispatched from Ayr in 1652 to occupy Brodick Castle. This force was responsible for some of the additions to the original structure which can still be seen at the present day. They fought a number of minor skirmishes with locals at locations such as the Cat Stone, just north of Corrie, and in the woods around Brodick Castle, but no actions of major importance. By 1657, the Duchess of Hamilton had redeemed the forfeited land on Arran. In 1705, the Montgomerie lands in the north-west of the island were ceded to the Hamiltons, and in 1800 they finally obtained the former Stewart lands of Corriegills, leaving the Fullartons of Glencloy as virtually the only independent landowners on the island. Arran was at last entering a period of political stability after the upheavals and conflicts which had typified the previous five hundred years.

CHAPTER 6

The Old Farmers

It comes as something of a shock to realise that the cultural landscapes of Arran, with all the ancient monuments and spiritual links with the ancient Celtic heroes, are essentially products of the last two hundred years only, and that hardly a building on the island predates the 'Improving' movement associated with the agricultural revolution at the end of the eighteenth century. It is as though the island is all antiquity and no history! How this strange state of affairs came about will be dealt with in the next chapter, but in the meantime, what can we say about the way of life of the ordinary folk on the island, those who were too humble and too poor to be noticed by history, before the reorganisation of the countryside came about?

We are fortunate in Arran that despite the lack of old buildings, associated tools and other utensils of everyday life from the centuries before the 'Improving' movement swept across the nation, estate records, parish records and travellers' accounts of the time enable us to reconstruct much of the lifestyle of the crofters on the island. This had changed little over the centuries, having evolved only slowly since the time of the Viking presence. The life of the peasants was largely independent of the battles of the nobility, and even of national conflict, save when they were conscripted into armies for this or that campaign or battle. For centuries, their main concern was the land they farmed, the fish they could catch from the sea, and the survival of their families. Times were often very hard, and there was precious little time or inclination to lift their gaze towards the broader horizons of political organisation and national interests.

The best insight we have into life in Arran prior to the agricultural revolution comes from information collected by those who wanted to alter the existing way of life, and so needed information for planning purposes. Maps and records of Arran life were compiled among others by John Burrel, employed in 1766 by the trustees of the 7th Duke of Hamilton

The attractive little villages of the island have been used several times in the past as a backdrop for television programmes. Here Sir Harry Secombe is seen making a programme in the clachan of High Corrie.

to plan for the introduction of the 'New Farming' to the island, and by Robert Bauchop who surveyed the whole island in 1811 in preparation for the imminent introduction of land reoganisation. From these sources, together with some traces of old field boundaries and plough marks still to be seen today, it is possible to work out more or less what life was like at that time.

The System of Land Organisation

If we were able to board a time machine and be transported back to the seventeenth or eighteenth century, what would the landscape of Arran have looked like? In terms of hills, rivers and valleys there would be only minimal differences to the modern scene, but the way that the population was distributed and the look of the fields and pastures was a far cry from that of the present day. The present fields, hedges, roads, villages and farmhouses would not exist. In place of the regular fields separated by hedges and occasional woods and coppices there would have been an open landscape, ploughed, sown and harvested as communal fields worked by the people of the local settlement. These fields would not have been enclosed by hedge or dyke. Thus the lush tinge that the hedges give to the present landscape would have been absent, and the scene would seem to be much bleaker and less hospitable than that of today.

Villages such as Brodick, Lamlash and Whiting Bay did not exist then, and the main type of settlement was the fermtoun or clachan, a collection of cottages and steadings loosely gathered together and surrounded by a parcel of land which the inhabitants worked by a combination of individual and communal labour. The size of these settlements can be gauged from the fact that Burrel's surveys of 1773 place 99 'farms' on the Hamilton estate, supporting a total of 1,110 families. Some of these 'farms' were especially large, one at Sliddery having a population in the 1770s of over 300 people.

Each of the clachans would have had a social structure. In its simplest form, the people of the clachan worked as a community, often organised by an individual who was also the tacksman, who paid a rent for the farm lands to the estate, and who in turn collected rent from each of the families in the clachan. The amount of rent paid to the tacksman was determined originally by the number of cattle owned by each family, though later it is thought that the system reversed, and each family was allowed to keep stock only to the limit of the amount of rent paid. Each family's share of the land was in proportion to the amount of rent they paid, and that share was allocated in terms both of grazing land and arable land. The right to a share of the land was heritable, but the actual land itself did not belong to any individual, but rather was distributed anew each year, probably by the drawing of lots.

The land held by each clachan would be divided and worked as three basic units. The first of these, the infield, comprised the land closest to the clachan buildings, was regularly manured with dung and seaweed, and was cultivated every year. Surrounding this was the second unit, known as the outfield, which was cropped on a sort of rota. It was ploughed

Although mild, winters in Arran are still too fierce to allow early lambs such as this one, born before Christmas 1987, to spend their first days of life in the great outdoors.

for crops until the crop yield dropped to a point where it was no longer considered worth planting again, then it was left fallow for a while or used as grazing before being returned to the plough. Beyond this was the communal pasture, often hill pasture, on which the farm stock were grazed.

The arable land was ploughed using a system known as 'run-rig', derived from the Gaelic 'roinn' — 'a share'. In this, the land was ploughed in such a way that soil was thrown in towards the centre of a rig (ridge) during both uphill and downhill ploughing, thereby causing a large ridge to be built up. Once a large enough ridge had been created, then the ploughman would change direction so as to start throwing soil up to form a new ridge parallel to the first and separated from it by a marked furrow which aided drainage. Eventually the whole of the arable land to be worked in a given year would be ploughed in this way.

The rigs were the basic unit used in the allocation of land to each of the families in the clachan. The actual allocation of individual strips was done by lot, usually on an annual basis, so that no family could keep all the best land for itself. Indeed the land that each family had was likely to take the form of rigs scattered across the 'infield' and that part of the 'outfield' that was in arable use. All the labour on the strips was a communal responsibility — each farmer would work on other patches of land as well as his own, though the produce of each rig belonged to the family which 'owned' it that year. The main crops would have been oats, barley, peas, beans and, after the seventeenth century, potatoes. Some flax was grown as well.

Cattle were the most important livestock, virtually being regarded as units of currency for the determination of shares of grazing land. Sheep, horses, and some goats were also reared, but pigs were very rare. Most of the clachans were near the coast, and the families could supplement their diet by fishing — cod, whiting, herring and a range of other fish including the huge sailfish being caught in the waters around the island. The fish would be salted or dried and some was sold on the mainland, along with cattle and horses, salt butter, flax and fishing nets made by the 'farmers'. In 1772, sale of herring from Arran amounted to some £300, while nets and flax each brought about £100 to the island economy. By 1793, herring sales had risen to £1,000, while cattle, usually taken to market in Ayrshire or Greenock, were worth some £1,200 annually.

The Decay of the Runrig System

One of the advantages of the runrig system as originally practised was that because there was no telling which strips of land a family might be allocated for the following year, there was every incentive to keep the land from becoming exhausted. By the eighteenth century it had become more common for each farm to be rented by a group of tenants, often more than ten, who paid the rent, and who had, as a lower social level within the clachan, a number of cottars and servants. These cottars paid nothing towards the rent of the farm, but gave labour to their superiors in return for the right to the produce from part of a rig. These additional mouths to feed led to more pressure on the land, and an extension of the rigs to new and less suitable areas. This had the result of dragging down the level of productivity a family could expect from its allocation of rigs, making the problem worse.

At about the same time, pressures from the estate to introduce farming reforms along the lines of those proposed by Burrel caused more change in the runrig system as practised on Arran. Burrel proposed the separation of upland pasture from arable land by the building of a head dyke. The land below that dyke was to be divided into 250 farms, each of which was to be a self-contained entity held by a single tenant and which did not have access to common pasture. Each lease was to be for 19 years only. This was a most radical proposal, a complete change from the system of communal runrig and clachan.

Burrel's efforts were to fail. Among the reasons was the fact that some 850 families would be put off the land, with no alternative source of significant employment on the island to absorb the labour. In contrast there would have been a shortage of implements and horses to work the individual farms, as these were held communally in the clachans, of which there were only 99 — not nearly enough to supply 250 farms with animals and tools.

None the less Burrel's ideas were to make an impact on runrig in Arran, because the estate tried to start reforming the system of tenure as a step towards implementing his ideas. The 19-year lease was introduced, and where there were multiple tenants, often they had their own subtenants, with whom they worked communally, but not with all the other tenants and their subtenants. Thus each 'farm' became rather more like part of a series of small independent yet intertwined farms. In 1792, the period of leases was reduced, sometimes to as little as three to five years, encouraging farmers to exploit the land rather than look after it.

The runrig system, already in decay, was to change still further with the development of individual tenants beginning to work only their own rigs. As these were usually widely scattered with the 'farm' lands, this led to very inefficient farming indeed, and a number of visitors to the island around the end of the eighteenth century were to comment on neglect of pastures, poverty and lack of spirit of the farmers of Arran at the time when improvements in agriculture were already widely adopted on the mainland, especially in Ayrshire. In this respect the island was still more Highland than Lowland in character, and it was not until 1815, when wholesale enclosure took place, that this rather depressing situation began to change.

Traces of runrig persisted in some remote parts of the island into the twentieth century, most notably at Balliekine (NR 870396) where runrig ended without any consolidation of holdings, so that the tenants simply kept the rigs last allocated to them. This gave rise to tiny fragmented holdings such as are found still in some parts of continental Europe.

The main relics of runrig cultivation still visible on Arran are the rigs themselves, parallel ridges of soil running downhill, which are still preserved on steeper slopes not taken in when enclosure finally came. Rigs can be seen in many parts of the island, such as the raised beach just north of Dougrie Lodge (NR 880372), along the banks of Sliddery Water at Bennecarrigan (NR 946242), Levencorroch (NS 007216) and Bennan Head (NS 001212). In these and several other places in Arran, the best time to pick out the old rigs is evening, when the low angle of the sun throws shadows from the rigs onto the hillslope so that they are clearly visible.

The Lot of the Common Man

A number of clachans can still be seen at the present day, for example at Shannochie (NR 979213), Shedog (NR 912301), Sliddery (NR 931229), Mayish (NS 016358), High Corrie (NS 022423) and Mid Thundergay (NR 881467). They can be distinguished by the rather haphazard way the houses are sprinkled over the ground, very different from the neat geometric patterns and rows of the 'new' villages that were to be built in the nineteenth century.

The buildings themselves are much more recent than the settlements. To judge from Bauchop's maps of 1811, many cottages are still standing where the clachan cottages stood, but the architecture of those cottages indicates that they were built within the last 150 years. The late Horace Fairhurst, a noted expert on the history and archaeology of Arran, considered that there was not a single house on Arran (other than the castles) which predated the 'Improvements' and the Enclosure movement. All that we know of how the inhabitants of the clachans lived has been gained by looking at the ruins of clachans in places like Gargadale (NR 957262), and by assuming a similar lifestyle to that practised elsewhere in the Highlands at that time.

It is likely that the basic house design changed little over centuries, and would have been very similar to the Hebridean 'blackhouse'. The walls were of dry-stone construction using a rubble core, and lined on the interior with packed clay. Heather or straw would have been the roofing material, supported on a system of poles. While there would have been windows to give light to the interior, glass would have been a rarity and shutters would have been the usual way of excluding the wind.

The size of cottage varied. Large ones may have been as much as twenty-five metres long by five to six metres wide. These would have belonged to the tenant farmers, while the cottars would have had rather smaller and still more primitive dwellings. The typical tenant's house would be divided into three rooms — a kitchen/living area, an inner room and a byre, in which the cattle and horses would be kept. The cooking was done on an open hearth in the kitchen. The inner room would be used for beds, though some kind of a loft could sometimes provide a place for the children of the household to sleep.

Such primitive kitchen conditions meant that little could have been done in the way of fancy cooking, even if the ingredients had been available. In fact, the diet typically was basic and derived almost entirely from the farm itself plus fishing activities. Typical foods would have been meal, potatoes, butter, cheese, eggs, dried mutton and salt fish (usually herring). The meal would be derived from grain grown on the farm, but it would often have been milled at a central facility on the estate. In 1811, Bauchop mapped five meal-mills, the Lamlash one standing beside what is now the site of the Arran Provisions factory at the foot of the Monamore Glen (NS 020301). This mill, which was water-driven, did not close until the early part of the twentieth century. The building itself stood until 1967, when it was demolished, as it had become unsafe.

The main source of fuel for cooking and heating would have been peat, which could be cut on the upland plateaux or on Machrie Moor. Old (and modern) peat cuttings are also known from the Boguillie, the high pass between Lochranza and Sannox, from which Arran Estates still control the extraction of peat. On the Boguillie there could also be seen the traces of old field boundaries in areas which are now moor and bog. These traces are rapidly disappearing under the spread of afforestation in this part of the island, but their presence in such an inhospitable place is a clear indication of the pressure there was for farm land on Arran two centuries ago.

The farmers would have spoken Gaelic. No native Gaelic-speakers are found on the island nowadays, and the decay of the language was evident as early as 1712, when parish records suggest that Kilmorie parish (the western half of the island) was largely bilingual, although the Gaelic was predominant. The change towards English would have been even earlier on the east coast of the island, the main area of contact with the mainland.

The demise of the Gaelic coincided with the spread of education on the island, for teaching was conducted in English. As early as 1805, there were at least ten schools on Arran, located in the main centres of population. The influence of the church was very strong here, for the schools were parish schools and the predominant feeling of the time was that the Gaelic was a heathen tongue, and the speaking of it was a contributory factor to the poverty and squalor in which most of the parishioners lived. English, on the other hand, was viewed as the gateway to a better, and more Christian, way of life.

The Non-Agricultural Economy

Mention has already been made of the fishing carried on by Arran 'farmers' and fishermen, but other, rather less legal, uses for boats were found which helped to augment the meagre income of the island. Naturally, smuggling was rife, particularly when customs duties were imposed on such goods as tobacco, spirits, malt and salt. The salt tax, introduced in

1702 and raised ultimately to a level which was thirty to forty times the primary cost of the product, led to huge profits for those willing to import it without customs inspection.

In 1725, the imposition of a duty on malt led to a vast decline in the production of home-brewed ale, and the increase in popularity of gin and brandy, both of which were carried to the Ayrshire ports in the same vessels that brought consignments of claret and other French wines for consumption in the towns and cities of the mainland. What could have been more natural to the adventure-loving Arranachs than to go out to meet the ships before they reached port, unload these spirits, both of which carried heavy excise duties, into their small boats and row them ashore on Arran? They could then be carried to the mainland and sold without ever troubling the clerks of the Customs and Excise.

The other clandestine industry, and one which again involved the smuggler, was the illegal distilling of whisky and rum, the latter apparently being produced from treacle. There were licensed distilleries on the island at the end of the eighteenth century, but not enough whisky was being produced to absorb the barley crop, so a little bit of free enterprise began to surface. There are no records to show the extent of illegal distilling on the island, but it is known that enough was made for the product to be exported, usually to the Ayrshire mainland at dead of night by local men. As far as can be determined, smuggling was virtually endemic in some parts of the island, especially the south coast around Kildonan and in Kilmorie parish, where it was considered an honourable occupation by all except the Revenue.

Tobacco smuggling was based on a rather different approach. A certain John Hamilton appeared before the kirk session in Kilmory parish in 1711 on a charge of loading tobacco from a bonded warehouse in Glasgow after having given his word that the cargo was for export and would not be landed anywhere in Britain. The temptation obviously was too great, for the records indicate that the tobacco got no farther than the Little Cumbrae where it was unloaded ready to be taken back to the mainland for sale. We do not know the final judgement, but we do know that John Hamilton was suspended from his position as church elder for the duration of the investigation.

Not all smuggling was treated in such a relaxed fashion. In 1754, three Arran men went on trial at the High Court in Edinburgh on charges of attacking customs officers at Lamlash and thereby obstructing them in the execution of their duty. They were found guilty and sentenced to banishment to America, still in British hands at that time.

Rather safer employment could have been found in the island's iron 'bloomeries' during the sixteenth and seventeenth centuries. These used iron ore, probably bog iron, plus ironstone which is known to outcrop on the lower Rosa Burn, along the shore near Corrie and at the Cock of Arran in the extreme north of the island. Locally the main fuel source was charcoal derived from the local forests. It is likely that this industry ceased largely as a result of exhaustion of the supply of suitable local wood.

The locations of a number of these old bloomeries are known on the island, and in some their existence is indicated by the presence of dumps of slag from the smelting. At Coillemore, Lochranza (NR 925508), an area of slag lies about thirty metres above sea-level, while at Glenkiln (NS 015304) by Lamlash other bloomery sites have been found. There seem also to have been iron-smelting works on the hill between Glen Shurig and Glen Cloy, just behind Brodick, around Whiting Bay at Largiebeg and at Kilpatrick, near Blackwaterfoot, among others. More interesting still is the reputed existence of a copper-smelting bloomery near Auchareoch (NR 993246), while silver is supposed to have been found in Glen Shurig (NR 990366), and even gold is said to have been extracted near Brodick.

Despite these outlets for employment (legal or not), the vast majority of the population of Arran at the end of the eighteenth century lived in the clachans, in poorly maintained housing, often badly overcrowded and with constant problems over health and wealth. At the same time as population pressure was affecting the physical well-being of the population, the erosion of their Gaelic culture was starting with the spread of formal education. It is little wonder that the Hamiltons sought to try and halt the decline in their estate lands and workers by drastic means, and it is only slightly more surprising that their objectives were achieved relatively rapidly, as we shall see.

CHAPTER 7

Enclosure and Clearance

The neat parcels into which agricultural land on Arran is divided today are very like similar neat parcels to be seen just across the water in Ayrshire and other parts of the West of Scotland. This landscape is so different from the one that Burrel saw on his early visits to the island around 1770, so essentially Lowland in superficial appearance, that the change can only have come about by revolution rather than evolution. This revolution is most evident in the southern half of the island and around Lochranza, in areas where there was reasonably fertile ground and enough of it for the laying out of regular fields. Probably the clearest example of this can be seen by looking west from the Ross Road near Bennecarrigan Farm (NR 942225) towards Corriecravie. The neat fields, clearly delimited by verdant hedgerows, are testimony to the influence of a 'civilising' hand on what had previously been a rather chaotic but essentially Highland vista.

The Arran 'farmscape' changed from the old runrig system to the modern enclosed system over rather a long time, at least compared with adjacent parts of the mainland. The first steps were taken by Burrel in the latter part of the eighteenth century, though the reality came nowhere near fulfilling his rather detached and academic plan. Burrel drew up schemes to reduce the number of farms on the ducal lands to 250, each held by a single tacksman who was to work the land on his own or with the aid of his family and possibly a cottar or two. Common grazing was to be abolished, the boundaries of each farm unit having been drawn up to include a range of lands from moor right down to sweet and fertile pasture and ploughland. The enclosed farmlands were to be separated from the moors by a stone or turf wall, the head-dyke, which formed a continuous barrier separating improved land from those areas on which sheep (now beginning to replace cattle) were to be grazed by the estate.

Tenants were to be forbidden to collect seaweed from the shores without prior permission from the Duke of Hamilton.

This was a major problem for the tenants, as such weed had traditionally been spread on the rigs as a fertiliser. Now the tenants were to be deprived of one of their main resources and the quality of the soil was to suffer as a result.

Burrel's schemes were to fail. Although holdings were amalgamated according to his plan, and the head-dyke built in many areas, the rents were too high for individuals to afford, so many of the new farms remained in multiple tenancies, and little or no land was enclosed. Burrel hoped to persuade people to leave the land by attempting to plant the idea of alternative employment using other resources on the island.

Fishing was practised around the coasts of the island, but it was not until 1787 that a bounty system designed to encourage fishermen was extended to include inshore fisheries such as those of the waters of the Firth of Clyde. The iniquities of the prohibitive salt tax meant that the preserving of such catches as the fishermen managed to make was rather inefficient, and so much of the catch had to be consumed on the island rather than be exported. An attempt was made to get round this by producing salt locally. Coal was mined at the Cock of Arran (NR 973512) and used to evaporate sea water in salt pans on the coast there. Some of the old mine shafts still exist, making it important for walkers in the area to watch where they place their feet. Attempts were also made at this time to exploit local reserves of limestone and slate, but these soaked up only a few of the displaced farmers.

That other traditional refuge of those people pushed off the land — emigration — was not really available. The fact that Britain and America were then engaged in the War of Independence virtually eliminated that possibility. The only alternative for many people was to move to the mainland but even that did not absorb many at this time, and by Burrel's calculation the population of the island in 1772 must have been over 7,000, a figure which he considered far more than the island could comfortably support. The problem was somewhat reduced by increasing consumption of the potato, which grew excellently on the light sandy coastal soils of the island. More people could be fed from a reduced acreage of cultivation, but even so it was difficult to produce enough food locally to feed all the population.

The Enclosures — Redrawing the Map of Arran

The next major 'expert' to cast an eye over Arran's agriculture was the Revd J. Headrick, a mineralogist and agriculturalist who arrived in 1807. In the main, his ideas were in line with those of Burrel, save that he advocated the setting up of grandiose industrial schemes with a view to absorbing the population which would be displaced upon the proper enclosure of the farms. He also favoured the use of the moors for sheep, although cattle were to be confined below the head-dyke. This decision, together with the adoption of the practice of burning the heather to encourage new shoots to grow, reduced ground disturbance and allowed the spread of bracken over much of the lower ground of Arran, stifling pasture and forming a marvellous breeding ground for the prolific Highland midge.

The real reorganisation of the land was started by the Duke of Hamilton in 1815, when strong encouragement was given to start enclosure. Though the process was to go on for several decades, probably reaching its peak in 1837, the momentum of the revolution was irresistible, and the open farmlands covered with rigs steadily shrank before a gathering tide of hedgerows and new farmhouses. By 1837, the ducal estate had been split into 448 holdings, the majority of which were very small, though some were quite large. The majority of the small farms were near to the coast in the southern half of the island. The tenants had to build houses, fence and enclose the land, and obey certain restrictions as to livestock. For example, the keeping of goats was banned, but pigs became more common. In return, the tenant was furnished with hedge plants, timber and lime being supplied also for the building of houses.

When the leases from the first round expired, a number of properties were amalgamated to form farms of 1 to 400 acres. These farms were not worked by locals, but farmers from districts on the mainland were brought in, bringing with them the knowledge of other new procedures which had not yet reached Arran. In a way, this was an imposition of a new 'aristocracy', reminiscent in a way of the so-called 'white settlers' of the modern-day island.

The last area of Arran to be enclosed was the north-west,

where an area had been ceded by the 8th Duke of Hamilton as a marriage dowry for his daughter Anne. This consisted of the coastal strip from Auchagallon Farm (NR 894347) to Catacol, and here the old runrig system persisted until the lands were returned to Hamilton hands around 1844.

The enclosures meant that fewer people could live on the land, but fortunately at this time changes in the outside world allowed more employment alternatives than had previously been available on the island. Tax changes meant that the local fishing industry was now profitable, and herring in particular were caught and sold to the mainland. The kelp industry, a source of soda, was also in a state of boom at the end of the eighteenth century because of cutting of European sources of soda as a consequence of war between Britain and France. Several farmers displaced by the enclosures moved to the coast where they lived in smallholdings, of which a number had been established by the estate. The beginning of the industrial revolution and the expansion of manufacturing industry on the mainland provided another outlet for those put off the land. Lastly, the ending of the American War of Independence opened up the possibility of emigration to the New World, though this was not a step that appealed to many at this time.

Sheep and Silence — the Arran Glens

Although the population of Arran was holding relatively steady now, because of migration to the mainland, another crisis was to surface in the 1820s. The coastal settlements based on fish, kelp and potatoes were already somewhat overpopulated. The ending of the Napoleonic Wars, and the subsequent lifting of trade barriers which allowed European soda to be imported to Britain, led to the collapse of the kelp industry, throwing more people out of work. The forces of emigration were beginning to gather momentum.

The largest push was to come from the spread of sheep-farming. The profits to be gained from wool and sheep-meat were such that the economics of keeping some of the small tenant farmers on marginal farmlands were very dubious, and all over the Highlands people were removed from their homes,

Bracken infestation, as here on the slopes of Glen Chalmadale near Lochranza, has become a major problem of Arran farming. The loss of pasture and good moorland grazing to the ravages of this plant are thought to date from the time of the enclosures of farmland in the eighteenth and early nineteenth centuries.

often forcibly. Fortunately little blood seems to have been shed in this cause on Arran. Nevertheless, those people who were put off the land were not keen to go, so that the events are still regarded as part of the 'Clearances'.

In the interior glens of the south, especially in the valleys of Sliddery Water and Kilmory Water, leases for the small farms obtained during the first round of enclosures were not renewed, and the farmlands were cleared to make way for sheep. People from there left the island, many of them going to Chaleur Bay in eastern Canada. All that is left to remind us of these people is the ruins of their homes, most notably the clachan of Gargadale (NR 957262) clearly visible from the Ross Road between Lamlash and Sliddery. The sight of sheep grazing in and around the ruins of the homes of the people they displaced is an evocative reminder of the trials of the common man in Arran.

More famous, probably because it is better chronicled, is the eviction of people from the Sannox area in the north-east of the island. This came about as a result of the clearance of North Glen Sannox and the area around Laggan and the Cock of Arran for sheep in 1829. The settlement in North Glen Sannox was possibly one of the largest in Arran at the time, and the ruins of the village can be seen quite clearly from the main road through North Glen Sannox (NS 000469) as scatters of stones on a low terrace on the north side of the burn. The population of the area must have been over 100, but after the clearance all that was left was a sheep farm which is now North Sannox Farm (NS 010466) and another smaller farm at the Cock.

A number of the displaced families found a living elsewhere on the island, or moved to the mainland. However, over 100 people eventually decided to take up an offer of assisted passage to Canada, the Duke of Hamilton having said that he would pay half the fare. On 25 April 1829, eighty-six of the former inhabitants of Sannox set sail for Canada in the brig *Caledonia,* an event commemorated by the monument on the green in front of Hamilton Terrace in the centre of Lamlash (NS 026311). Other families followed within a couple of months, and in all 114 former residents of North Glen Sannox ended up in the Megantic area of Quebec.

It is worth noting that the people of the Sannox area were among the most strictly religious of the inhabitants of Arran. When a mission by the Haldane brothers arrived in 1800, preaching a fundamentalist view of the gospels, it was in Sannox that they made the deepest impression. The fanaticism that this produced was to surface again in Kilmory parish in 1815, when the parishioners objected to the minister whom the Duke of Hamilton presented as the successor to the previous incumbent who had recently died. The dispute over this patronage, which led ultimately to a breakaway movement which for six years held services in a cave on the shore just below Kilpatrick (NR 900266), was ultimately to result in the creation of the separate Free Church of Scotland in 1843. The Arran emigrants to Canada, although predating the formal creation of that Church, were adherents of the same strict beliefs. These beliefs were to lead to one of the main disagreements to affect the settlers in Megantic County.

The winters in that part of Canada are very much colder than anything the Arranachs had experienced before, and presented them with problems of a completely unforeseen

This monument in Lamlash commemorates the departure of the crofters cleared from North Glen Sannox in 1829, and their embarkation on the first step of the long journey to Canada.

type. The old Arran Sabbath was one in which no work at all was done, not even cooking or drawing water from wells. Water would be drawn on the Saturday for use the next day. The problem in Canada was that in winter the water froze overnight in the vessels in which it was stored, causing them to break. The only way round this was to draw water on the Sabbath, a procedure which gave rise to prolonged argument in the little settlement, the 'modernists' eventually winning the day and conceding that at least one aspect of the traditional Arran Sabbath would have to be left behind in the Old World!

The irony of the whole subject of the clearances in Arran was that the boom in sheep products lasted for only a short while. Eventually the economics of sheep farming became less favourable for the estate owners than those of turning mountain and moorland into deer forest. The growth of sporting estates was given a huge boost by Queen Victoria's acquisition of Balmoral on Deeside, and it became extremely fashionable to hunt and fish in Scotland. The 11th Duke of Hamilton, too, began to develop Arran for the benefit of those who could afford the 'sporting life', and the shooting lodges at

Dippen (NS 050223) and Dougrie (NR 884372) were built to help develop this early version of tourism.

The red deer had been hunted to such an extent that Arran supported only a few tens of beasts by the end of the eighteenth century. In 1859, the Duke imported fresh stags from the mainland with a view to revitalising the local stock, having already organised a deer park at Brodick Castle. Since then, the numbers of deer have risen steadily.

The interest in red deer also provoked the last of the Arran clearances. The clachan of Old Catacol (NR 918490) was cleared to make way for the deer. In this case, though, the estate had built new houses for the inhabitants. This row of small cottages, known popularly as the 'twelve Apostles', forms the main part of the modern hamlet of Catacol (NR 912497), and features picturesquely on many postcards of Arran. However, they did not appeal to those for whom they were originally intended. The former inhabitants of Old Catacol refused to live in them, preferring instead to move to other parts of the island. The cottages, nowadays snapped up as second homes for the most part, were to stand empty for at least two years before tenants could be found for them.

The Integration of the Island Communities

At the beginning of the eighteenth century, Arran was not only somewhat isolated from the mainland, but also there was a degree of internal isolation as well. At that time, the majority of the population lived in the west of the island, but links between the west and the east were not good, although there were some drove roads along which cattle were driven on their way to be sold on the mainland. Their remains can still be seen in Gleann ant-Suidhe (NR 970356) and in Glen Chalmadale (NR 960493), where they take the form of broad paths on the opposite side of the glen to that taken by the modern road.

Drove roads were all very well, but a leisurely walk behind a herd of cattle is rather different from rapid transport by wheeled vehicle. For a long time, wheeled traffic on the island was rendered useless by the total absence of suitable roads, and the easiest way to get about was on horseback or by boat.

Dairy cattle like this Jersey cow on a farm near Machrie supply the island with milk and cheese.

Gradually, however, a system of surfaced roads appeared on the island.

All tenants had to provide the estate with six days labour a year, and this muscle power was used in the early nineteenth century to build roads on the island. By 1810, there was a road suitable for wheeled traffic from Gortonallister (NS 031298), south of Lamlash, to Brodick. By 1817, the road network had extended to include Brodick-Sannox and the String Road linking Brodick and Blackwaterfoot, the latter road being planned by the noted Scots engineer, Thomas Telford. The Ross Road, linking Lamlash with Sliddery, was built in 1821-22, as were a number of small roads in the Whiting Bay area. These roads were than gradually linked together, though it was not until 1843 that the Boguillie, linking Sannox and Lochranza, was constructed. The last road link to be completed on the island was the Craw, the road from Pirnmill to Catacol along the north-west coast of the island.

All the Arran roads presented problems to the engineer, running as they do over steep slopes, through narrow defiles and along exposed coasts, but the Craw was by far the most difficult, as this is almost the only place on the island where the mountains fall straight into the sea without a narrow ribbon of raised beach along which to place the road. The modern road is still bedevilled here by landslides and erosion by the sea, and has been forced up and over a series of blind humpback hills, known to me in my childhood as 'The Hiccups' from the feeling that you got in your stomach from travelling over them too fast while strapped into the back seat of a car!

These roads originated in improved communications with the island by sea, and the integration of Arran farms and produce into mainland markets. The development of ferries was a major factor, as not only could Arran produce go to the mainland, but merchants could come to Arran to purchase cattle and horses. Agricultural fairs were held at a number of locations on the island, horses being the chief items of trade at Lagg, Shedog and Lamlash, whilst Brodick was noted for cattle and wool sales, a role which it still carries on at the present day.

In Burrel's day there were no ferry services to Arran and he had to travel by hitching lifts on available vessels such as customs cutters. Local pressure, plus a brief fashion for coming to Arran to drink goat's milk (considered a health food at the time) meant that a packet service was instigated to link Brodick with Saltcoats in Ayrshire in 1770. The service was very much at the mercy of wind and tide and the unfortunate passengers were sometimes becalmed for a day or more en route! In the 1820s the packet boat network became better developed and more reliable thanks to the advent of steam. By the end of the decade, there were two steam packets a week from Glasgow to Brodick and Lamlash. Once the railway reached Ardrossan in the 1840s, it became the main point of departure for the island. At the same time the frequency of crossings rose to one a day in summer.

Sailing packets also linked other parts of the island to the mainland. An established crossing went from Blackwaterfoot to Campbeltown in Kintyre, while another irregular packet linked Whiting Bay with Ayr. These routes became less and less important over the years as the regular steam service from Brodick and Lamlash, eventually extended to include Whiting Bay, took over the vast bulk of the trade in farm produce and fish.

The annual Arran Show, held in Lamlash, features the cream of Arran livestock, including this champion Ayrshire cow. Such shows are a major focus for island social life.

One problem for the ferries was the lack of proper harbour or pier facilities on the island. People and goods had to be transferred to the shore in small boats, and accidents were not uncommon. There were quays at Corrie, Lamlash and Brodick (just below the castle), but none of these was large enough to take the steam packets. Elsewhere on the island natural harbours suitable only for the smallest of boats were the only possible landing places. The absence of a proper harbour is surprising, but according to the *New Statistical Account* of 1845 there had once been an excellent quay at Lamlash, but it had been demolished about 1800 and the stone used in the construction of Lamlash village. The foundations of this quay are traceable at low tide below the village green.

Part of the explanation for this piece of wanton vandalism, which greatly increased the inaccessibility of the island for a while, may lie in the attitude of the estate to the growing number of visitors to Arran in the summer. They appear to have been regarded as a potential menace if they became too numerous, especially as their presence made it more difficult to retain the island as a sort of exclusive game park for the rich and mighty. Locals were tolerated, as they provided useful labour and added a quaint rustic element to the scene. In other words, an attitude similar to that of some landowners in parts of the Highlands at the present day!

The desire for privacy and space to develop ideas was also behind the founding of the modern village of Brodick. In 1844, following the marriage of the 11th Duke of Hamilton to Princess Marie of Baden, a decision was taken to improve the castle policies and to make a deer park there. The old village of Brodick was substantially demolished to make way for these developments, though the clachan at Cladach (NS 012377) is a remnant of the original settlement, and includes, opposite the Home Farm, a cottage which was the Old Inn of Cladach.

The population of the Cladach was rehoused in purpose-built houses on the south side of Brodick Bay. These houses, which can still be seen in Douglas Place and Alma Terrace, formed the nucleus from which the present-day village of Brodick has grown. This was one of the earliest attempts to produce planned villages, designed to the estate's specification, on the island, and showed that even at the dawning of the Victorian era, the feudal attitude was far from dead on Arran.

CHAPTER 8

Victorian Arran

The nineteenth century was to see major changes in the island of Arran. Within those few decades the economy and the social structure of the island were to change from an open-field agricultural pattern to a situation where the island was dominated by the wealth produced by the new industrial era, although agriculture also had a part to play. Despite this, Arran was to remain almost immune from the evils of the spread of the 'dark satanic mills' and factories, reaping instead its benefits from social changes that these developments brought about. In particular, Arran was to benefit from the growth in holidays and tourism which were the by-product of this era. In a way there was a form of exchange, with much of the surplus population from the land moving to the cities in search of work, and the wealth they created enabling others (and sometimes themselves) to take their leisure in a place which could hardly be farther in atmosphere from the smoky industrial hells of the mainland.

Industrial Arran

Arran's popularity as a holiday resort may have stemmed from the lack of industrial scarring of the landscape, but that does not mean that the nineteenth-century mania for industrial development completely ignored the island. Over the years a number of industrial enterprises were set up. Most of these were based on the processing of local products to produce goods for consumption on the island itself. Many were to fail because the population of the island was to decline. It was too expensive to ship the goods to the mainland to sell, and indeed cheaper equivalent goods from the mainland could often be shipped to the island and undercut the local product. Traces of the attempts to plant industry on Arran can still be seen, but most of these enterprises have since been overwhelmed by the mists of history.

The most fundamental resources of the island are the rocks themselves. Attempts to mine coal for the manufacture of salt at the Cock of Arran, and to produce slate and limestone from local sources formed a significant element of the plan for the enclosure of the farmlands, as we have already seen. Most of these schemes were soon to founder, usually for economic rather than social reasons. The limestone resources gave rise to a rather longer-lived lime-burning industry, with kilns at Corrie, Shiskine and Clauchog, near Lagg. This last kiln was still in use in 1898, when there is a record of a load of limestone from Ireland being brought there by the owner in his own smack. Presumably the product was sold on the island, though why local limestone was not adequate for this purpose is unclear.

The main local sources for limestone were the Clauchan Glen, just north of Shiskine, and Corrie, where there are quarries on the hillslope immediately above the picturesque old harbour in the centre of the village (NS 025436). This quarrying went on at least until World War I, when Robert McLellan suggests that the focus of excavation had moved uphill to an area a little north-north-west of High Corrie, and the product conveyed by a tramway to the 'Sandstone Harbour' (NS 026428), from where it was transferred to ships and taken to the mainland.

White sandstone is another rock product formerly quarried near Corrie. The overgrown traces of some old quarries can be seen on the hillslopes above the village, while the Ferry Rock (NS 026434) on the foreshore a few yards north of the Corrie Hotel was the site of another quarry from which this hard, compact rock was extracted. Arran white sandstone was used in the building of the Crinan Canal in Argyllshire, and is also supposed to have been taken to the Isle of Man to make a harbour wall.

A number of quarries were started on Arran to exploit the reserves of red sandstone that are so widespread in the southern part of the island. Small local quarries supplied stone in Brodick, Cordon (NS 027301), the Monamore Glen just west of Lamlash, and at Corrie. In particular, red sandstone was the favoured building material when the 'new' villages of Brodick and Lamlash developed in the second half of the nineteenth

Some fishing villages on the more exposed coasts of Arran operated without a proper harbour. Instead, a winch like this one at Pirnmill was used to haul the boats up the beach and out of the reach of the waves.

century. Indeed most of the major houses, hotels and commercial buildings on the island display that distinctive reddish colour save where they have been harled or whitewashed.

The largest sandstone quarries on the island were at Corrie, and can be seen cutting into the fossil cliff just behind the local authority housing at the south end of the village (NS 025423). Corrie sandstone was of very good quality, and a considerable export market developed in it. Many of the sandstone houses of the Ayrshire coastal resorts, of Greenock, and of some parts of Glasgow, are built from it, as are the harbour wall at Troon, and Kinloch Castle on the island of Rhum. To facilitate this trade, the 'sandstone' or 'new' harbour at Corrie was built in 1882, and linked by a light railway to the quarries. The railway no longer exists, and the harbour fell into a degree of disrepair once the quarries finally closed in 1928. A great pile of sandstone blocks still stands on the harbour wall, waiting for the boat that will carry it away to be fashioned into a major piece of architecture. It will be a long wait, unless a major change in building fashions produces a renewed demand for this lovely warm-coloured stone.

A couple of miles north of Corrie, in Glen Sannox, can be seen some rather ugly areas of reddish 'spoil', together with the ruined stumps of what looks like a small factory. These mark the site of the barytes mining industry in Arran. Barytes is a mineral used in the manufacture of paint, as well as having a range of other uses and being a source of barium. A vein of the mineral runs north–south across the Sannox Water, and was exploited by a series of surface excavations and shallow shafts, the marks of which trace the line of the vein (NS 007453). It was first mined about 1840, and during the period 1853-62 some 500 tons of the mineral were produced. The enterprise was brought to a sudden halt by the 11th Duke of Hamilton, on the grounds that it was spoiling the grandeur of the scene, a conclusion with which most present-day conservationists would have great sympathy.

This did not mark the end of the enterprise, though, as mining was to start again in Glen Sannox in 1919. Production at the site was rather more efficient now than previously, aided by an on site crushing and screening plant (the ruins of which dominate the site at present), and a light railway which took the ore to the loading pier at the mouth of the Sannox Water (NS 018453). In 1934, 8,693 tons of barytes were produced, but then the vein began to peter out, and production ended in 1938.

The Fishing Industry

Traditional methods of farming always used seaweed as a fertiliser on the fields. With the enclosure of the lands this ceased, but a kelp industry grew at the end of the eighteenth century, supplying soda for the mainland. The collapse of this industry as a result of the lowering of trade tariff barriers in the 1820s threw some of the inhabitants of coastal settlements on Arran out of work, but the majority in places like Lochranza managed to scrape a living by a combination of fishing and working smallholdings.

Fish had been taken to the mainland and sold for centuries, but it was not until the extension of certain tax encouragements to inshore fishermen in 1787 that it became a large-scale industry. The waters around Arran were rich in fish, with herring, whitefish, lobster and crabs all being exploited by the local fishermen. Lamlash Bay was particularly noted for whitefish, while lobster and crab came from the south end of the island, and were taken to Glasgow for sale. But the main part of the Arran fisheries was concentrated on the herring, and in 1847 there were nearly 100 wherries in the local fleet. Fishing was concentrated in the Loch Fyne waters, famed for their herring, and which lay just to the north of Lochranza. It is thus not surprising that the bulk of the local fishing boats and fishermen came from the villages of the north-west of Arran, and in particular Lochranza, Pirnmill and Catacol.

Although Arran supported some larger fishing vessels which travelled as far afield as the Outer Hebrides, the bulk of the local fisheries were based on small boats. As the inshore waters became worked out, larger boats were needed, but harbour facilities for such boats were absent in Arran until the end of the nineteenth century. Capital was also required for curing and marketing facilities, and Arran simply could not compete with the larger mainland towns such as Ayr. As early as the 1840s the rich grounds off the south end of the island were being fished by boats from the mainland rather than from Arran, and local boats often had to land their catches on the mainland. Thus the Victorian era saw a major decline in fishing as an island industry, and by the beginning of the twentieth century it was virtually confined to Lochranza and Pirnmill.

Textile and Other Industries

The late eighteenth and early nineteenth centuries saw attempts to produce a textile industry on Arran, based on local wool and flax. There were carding mills at Brodick and at Burican in the south-west of the island, a flax mill at Lagg, and a wauking and dye mill at Monamore, near where the Ross Road joins the main road through Lamlash. All of these initiatives were to fail for economic reasons, particularly with the coming of steam power to the mainland competitors. Poor wee Arran simply didn't have the scale of production to compete with these mainland monsters!

One local industry that did profit from the industrial revolution was the supply of 'pirns' or bobbins to the cotton mills of Paisley. The manufacture of these gave rise to the modern name of the village in which they were produced — Pirnmill. The ruins of the mill can still be seen just behind the post office and tearoom in the centre of the village (NR 872442). The industry flourished from 1780 until 1840, when local supplies of suitable wood ran out.

It surprises many modern visitors to the island that there is not a distillery on Arran. This was not always the case. In 1793 there were three distilleries on the island, the last of which, Torrylinn (Lagg), seems to have closed in 1836. This meant that barley grown on the island to supply the whisky industry was now shipped to Campbeltown to supply distilleries there.

The only other industrial developments of any note around this period were the manufacture of clay drain tiles at Clauchog, near Lagg, and the milling of grain on the island. The tile manufacture ceased quite early because of exhaustion of local materials and the costs of transporting the product, but the meal mills persisted for a while. Bauchop's map of 1811 revealed five meal mills, but by 1878 there were only two — at Shedog and Monamore. These continued to operate until the 1920s.

The Coming of the Tourists

There is one very important industry that has not yet been mentioned in any detail. This is tourism, the first real stirrings of which began to be felt in the Victorian era. Tourism was ideal for Arran. The main resources required, scenery, tranquillity and sea air, were unlikely to be worked out in the way that the raw materials for other island industries had been. All that was needed was reasonable transport links between the island and the mainland, places to stay in on the island, people who had the resources to come to Arran on holiday, and publicity to let the world know of the joys of Arran. All of these were to come about during the nineteenth century, for a variety of reasons.

A Clyde puffer moored at the quay at Brodick. These little vessels provided one of the main lifelines to the island for most of this century, really only losing their role once vehicle ferries started to link Arran to the mainland.

The Growth of the Villages

At the beginning of the Victorian era, there were few signs of the modern villages that dot the coast of the island today. The population was both more scattered and rather greater than it is now, and it was not until enclosure of the land and clearance of settlements like that in North Glen Sannox in the early part of the nineteenth century that significant changes came about.

The first major developments took place in the 1850s, when the 11th Duke of Hamilton cleared most of the population of the old village of Brodick in order to improve the castle policies. The displaced people were rehoused in specially built estate cottages which can still be seen in Douglas Place and Alma Terrace. At the same time, Brodick primary school and a new hotel were built, the latter to replace the old inn at Cladach. This has evolved into the present-day Douglas Hotel, ideally situated to serve travellers arriving from the steamer, once a proper pier had been constructed on the south side of the bay in 1872.

This phase of building by the estate also saw the erection of the 'Twelve Apostles' at Catacol, and the lodges at Dippen and Dougrie. Schools were built at a number of locations on the island, and were later taken over, and their number added to, by the Parish School Boards which came into existence following the introduction of compulsory education through the Scottish Education Act of 1872. Several of these Victorian school buildings still survive on the island.

The second major wave of building took place in the last two decades of the century. Probably the best example of this estate housing is Hamilton Terrace in Lamlash, constructed in 1894 by the 12th Duke of Hamilton to rehouse people from a row of old cottages which had stood slightly closer to the sea. But it was not until the death of the 12th Duke, in 1895, that estate restrictions on building were released and feus much more readily granted. The result of these changes was a mushrooming of the east-coast villages in particular, with many of the villas, hotels and commercial properties being constructed at that time.

Lochranza in 1880 was mostly small croft houses around Colliemhor (near the present pier) and Narachan (NR 945502). The building of the main section of the village along the south shore of the loch took place around the end of the nineteenth century, mostly following on the authorising of the construction of the steamer pier in 1888. With the collapse of the fishing industry in the area, many of the men from the village left to join the merchant marine. By the end of the century there were nearly thirty people with Master Mariner's certificates in a village of less than 500 souls. With the loosening of controls on building, they invested in the construction of a number of substantial houses in the village. Other villas were built around the same time by wealthy mainland businessmen, a pattern repeated in those other villages on the island which had good steamer connections with the mainland.

The building of villas, such as those in Lochranza, represented just one strand of the tourist provisions which were beginning to appear. Although the main phase of hotel and boarding-house construction did not start until nearly the end of the nineteenth century, there had been some hotels on the island before that, in addition to the inn at Cladach. The

The Old Harbour at Corrie was once used to export limestone mined from the hillside above the port. Nowadays it caters only for pleasure craft.

Lagg Hotel may be as old as 1791, while the Kildonan Hotel dates from around 1800, though it is doubtful whether any of the present building is as old as that. The *New Statistical Account* of 1845 also makes mention of 'neat slated cottages' being built around Brodick Bay and offering accommodation to summer visitors.

Despite such provisions, the estate did not really welcome holidaymakers, except the well-heeled and well-connected who were welcome to come for the hunting and shooting facilities which it was thought would be spoilt by opening up the island to masses of visitors. Eventually, once the 12th Duke had been persuaded that without the extra income from visitors many of his tenants might be in need of support by the estate, it was decreed that visitors could be taken, provided that an increased rent was paid. From this sprang the real growth in cheap lodgings for summer visitors, both for boarders and as houses to let.

In wandering around the villages of the island, especially on the east coast, it is common to see houses with a small cottage in the garden ground, or with what appears to be a large extension built at the back. These are products of the relaxation of building regulations together with the new permission to take in lodgers on the island, and are known as 'double feus', in which two dwellings are built on the one plot of land. For most of the year, the smaller structure remained empty, but in summer the owner and family would move into it, leaving the main house empty for letting, a system that is in use even to the present day.

By the end of the century, catering for summer visitors had become so central to the economy of the island that in the most popular centres a number of special facilities were built to help make the island more attractive. Brodick village hall was built around 1895 to provide entertainment on wet days and in the evenings, a practice soon followed by other villages. Golf courses sprang up all over the island, with 18-hole courses at Lamlash, Brodick (though not the present site which was not brought into use until 1913) and the unique 12-hole course at Blackwaterfoot being in use in the 1890s, soon to be followed by others at Machrie and Whiting Bay. Arran was arriving in the age of tourism.

Transport to and on the Island

Almost throughout the Victorian period the population of the island was in decline. In 1841 it stood at 6,241, by 1861 it was reduced to 5,600, and by 1901 it had dropped still further to 4,900 despite slight in-migration being recorded in 1881 and 1891.

The age balance of the population also was to change, with significantly fewer children and more old people in 1881 than in 1841. The young active people were leaving an area of poor employment prospects, moving to mainland cities or emigrating, leaving the elderly and the infirm behind. This is the sort of pattern that can be seen in many parts of the Highlands today, where bodies such as the Highlands' and Islands Development Board are trying to fight depopulation by the use of subsidies and grants to small industries. In Arran, the rate of loss of young people dropped rapidly once the controls on letting of houses to visitors were relaxed, as now there could be employment and more money on the island.

The other aspect of the change in population was that the main growth of tourist provision was in the east-coast villages such as Brodick, Lamlash, Whiting Bay and Corrie, and only to a lesser extent in places like Blackwaterfoot, Lochranza and

Dougrie Lodge, a Victorian shooting lodge built by the Dukes of Hamilton to accommodate their guests during hunting parties, has a magnificent situation at the mouth of Glen Iorsa on the west coast of the island.

Pirnmill. When the figures for the individual parishes are investigated, it can be seen that Kilmory, the western parish, lost population far faster than Kilbride, and by the end of the century it contained less than half of the people of the island, the first time since records began that this had happened. This, remember, is despite the fact that Kilmory has a much higher proportion of the good arable land than Kilbride. Thus we can see that there must have been a huge change in the basis of the economy of Arran.

Why should those changes have affected the eastern villages more than the western ones? After all, there are many most attractive places in the western half of the island. The answer appears to lie in part with transport. The development of steam-packet boats to serve Arran brought about a transport revolution on the island. No longer did the passenger run the risk of being becalmed on the way to or from the island. Instead, departing from Glasgow, Greenock or Ardrossan, the visitor could feel confident of arriving on Arran within two or three hours, though not without some difficulty because of lack of piers at which steamers could dock. Everywhere the passengers and goods had to be transferred to smaller boats, usually propelled by oarsmen, who would ferry them ashore.

This operation was fraught with problems, and there must have been many an occasion when luggage or indeed passengers went for their first swim of the holiday rather earlier than intended! Villages served by such methods included Brodick, Lamlash, Whiting Bay, Blackwaterfoot, Lochranza (where the Ferry Rock where passengers disembarked is just to the west of the remains of the present pier), Pirnmill, King's Cross and Corrie (where the Ferry Rock lies just north of the Corrie Hotel).

The first proper pier on the island was built at Brodick in 1872 on the site of the present structure. Piers at Lamlash and Lochranza (where the ferry from Greenock to Campbeltown called) were built in the 1880s, and the last major pier, at Whiting Bay, was built in 1901. The piers were built in relatively sheltered bays at locations which helped to make the journey to the mainland as short (and hence as profitable for the steamer owners) as possible. The building of the piers coincided with the relaxation of rules on letting of houses, and the boom that followed was concentrated more around the villages served by piers than in the more remote areas. Thus places like Pirnmill, Kildonan and Blackwaterfoot began to lose population to the 'boom centres' of the east.

The waters of the Firth of Clyde were alive with steamers, mostly of the paddle variety, at the end of the nineteenth century. No modern-day monopolies here! The full story is too complex to be told here, but suffice it to say that rival steamer companies such as the Caledonian Steam Packet Company and the Glasgow and South Western Railway Company competed on the same route in much the same way as modern bus companies have done in cities like Glasgow since deregulation. These 'boat wars' were most prevalent on the services from Ardrossan to Whiting Bay, Lamlash and Brodick.

The result was that for a time Arran had probably the most intensive ferry service in its history. Paddles threshed the surface of the sea to foam and bow-waves built higher and higher as skippers raced each other to try to get to the pier ahead of their rivals, pick up all the waiting passengers and take the resultant profits. The companies put on more sailings per day to try and obtain a share of the market, at least in the summer months. There was even a temperance ferry, the *Ivanhoe*, which sailed from Helensburgh to Arran via Rothesay.

Competition reached such levels that in the summer of 1908, there may have been as many as eight steamers a day offloading passengers at places as small as King's Cross.

Roads were still poor, so that in the 1880s the fastest way from Whiting Bay to Brodick and Lamlash was by ferry, and for a while this helped to preserve the practice of offloading of passengers at places like Corrie, King's Cross and Pirnmill. As the roads improved, and public transport began to develop a network linking the villages without piers to those with them, the offloading began to die out, and the steamer schedules centred on the piers.

The first wagon to ply for hire on the island arrived about 1863, and was owned by a man named McBride in the Brodick area. (Mitchell-Lukers's *Arran Bus Book* suggests the date may have been much earlier, probably around 1820, which if correct would make it possibly the earliest known example of an omnibus service in Britain.) One John Davidson then introduced a regular two-horse carriage service between Brodick and Corrie in 1870, occasionally extending his range to cross the String or the Boguillie. It is said that on these latter occasions he had to take a third horse, to act as a relief animal on some of the steeper stretches.

In 1878, a coach run started, linking Corriecravie and Lamlash, while in 1879 a regular mail coach service was introduced by Ernest Ribbeck, one of two German brothers who had arrived on the island in the days of Princess Marie of Baden — to paint the gates of Brodick Castle according to one story — and who became postmaster in Brodick in 1871. The Ribbeck family still have an interest in transport on the island, and Ribbeck's Garage is situated to this very day in the centre of Brodick village.

By 1880 there was a further service linking the Kildonan Hotel with Whiting Bay, while around the same time services from Machrie to Brodick and Machrie to Lochranza were introduced by Charles Weir of Machrie. By 1890, the south coast of the island was also served by a coach from the Lagg Hotel to Whiting Bay, and Colin Currie of Shiskine had established a mail and passenger service between Shiskine and Brodick (fare two shillings), extended in 1893 to include Blackwaterfoot. Thus by the turn of the century a well-

integrated network of public transport linked the outlying
parts of the island with the steamers.

The Arran Visitors

During the Victorian era, Arran gradually changed from an
island essentially cut off from the mainland, and visited only by
the odd adventurer or member of the aristocracy looking for
sport, to a place with relatively easy access from the mainland,
and providing a wide range of accommodation and
entertainments. It is interesting to see how the nature of the
visitors changed during this period.

In the eighteenth century, Arran received visitors from the
mainland mainly in response to a fashion for the drinking of
goat's milk for health purposes. An advertisement in the
Glasgow Journal of 12 March 1759 indicated that such milk was
to be had in a house near to Brodick Castle, and gave details of
boats to the island from Saltcoats.

Early publicity for the wonders of Arran began to appear in
the form of literary works. Sir Walter Scott used the island as a
backdrop in his epic poem of 1814, *The Lord of the Isles*. This
publication, coinciding to some extent with a growing public
interest in scenery as a backdrop to romantic deeds, must have
encouraged some people to visit the scene of the tale.

Further publicity was given to Arran in 1828 by the Revd Dr
David Landsborough who published a poem about the island.
This he followed in 1843 with a book entitled *Excursions in
Arran, with Reference to the Natural History of the Island*. In the
1870s his son, also Revd David Landsborough, published a
book of writings by his father and by himself about the island.
These formed the first real tourist guide to Arran, and the
things they suggested that the visitor could do — walking,
fishing, climbing and swimming — show that the attractions of
the island have changed little over time.

Among more noted visitors at this time were the poet, Robert
Browning, who stayed at Blairbeg, Lamlash (NS 024315) in
1862. It is known that he came to visit a family called Hering,
who lived in Brodick in the house that is now the Ormidale
Hotel (NS 012358). The Herings were a family of German
origin who knew Princess Marie of Baden, wife of the 11th
Duke of Hamilton. They were to adopt a little girl in Brodick,

A workshop manufacturing quality leather bags on Arran for sale both there and in a shop in Edinburgh. This is just one example of the specialist crafts and products which have broadened and strengthened the employment base on the island in the last decade.

reputed to be the illegitimate daughter of the Duke by a local girl, and they named her Jeanie. Certainly, the Duke built Ormidale for the family about this time, a gesture which is easy to understand if the tales about Jeanie's real parents were true. Jeanie was to inherit Ormidale, which became a summer home for her and her husband, an extremely successful portrait sculptor who worked mainly within high London society. It was through Jeanie that a number of the 'top people' in London came to hear of the glories of Arran.

Sir Noel Paton, Queen Victoria's Limner for Scotland, stayed many a summer in Arran, renting a house each time. Among his noted visitors when in residence was Charles Dodgson, better known as Lewis Carroll, who visited him in 1871 in Lamlash.

Herbert Asquith, who became Prime Minister a few years before the start of World War I, was another noted visitor. His opinion that Corrie was the prettiest village in Europe is a little surprising in that his first wife died of typhoid contracted while renting a house on the island. She is buried in the Kilbride graveyard at Lamlash.

It may appear that Victorian Arran was an exclusive playground for the rich and famous, and this is indeed true to some extent. The relatively lengthy journey time needed to get there from any of the major industrial centres, even after the coming of the railway to Ardrossan in 1840, meant that day trips were costly and difficult, and the tripper market never really developed at all. Even if manual workers had bothered to come on such a journey, Arran had no organised entertainment after the fashion of places like the Ayrshire resorts or Rothesay, nor did it have many cheap lodgings close by the piers in which such people might just have been able to afford to stay. Instead, it catered for the middle classes with a sprinkling of aristrocracy, in particular for businessmen and their families from the city. Many of them built their own villas on the island once building restrictions had been relaxed, while the others rented houses or stayed in one of the numerous 'genteel' small hotels which sprang up at this time.

The professional classes formed the bulk of Arran visitors at that time, as indeed they still do to some extent. The style and expense of a late-Victorian holiday on the island must have been something to which many aspired but relatively few could manage. It was common for the wealthy to bring their entire household, including servants, on holiday. A large house would be taken for the whole summer, for the frantic competition for steamer traffic had produced a timetable which allowed the husband to commute from the island to places like Glasgow and Paisley. By taking the first steamer, it was possible to be at work by 10am, and to be back on the island by 6 or 7 after a day's work! A variant of this can be found in some families at the present day, who rent a house for a month, the husband taking two weeks' proper holiday, and then going to stay on the mainland through the working week and returning to Arran for the weekends.

This style of holiday, in which the essential ingredients were peace, fresh air and a comfortable place to stay, established Arran as a different kind of holiday centre from the rather urban, noisy and thronged resorts elsewhere on the Firth of Clyde. This difference was seen as part of the charm of the place, reflecting a typical British class segregation even on holiday. Although the barriers are breaking down to some degree nowadays, Arran's clientèle is still basically the same now as it was in Victorian days.

CHAPTER 9

Twentieth-Century Arran

There can be little doubt that the visitor to Arran nowadays sees a very different island in many respects from that which could have been seen at the end of the Victorian era. Although remote in some respects, and insulated from the effects of the more extreme and short-lived fluctuations of fashion, the island and its life have become increasingly integrated with the mainland. Modern visitors will still find much to delight them, but they will not have to suffer from any lack of 'mod cons' during their stay on Arran.

In the nine decades of the twentieth century, Arran has experienced the ravages of two world wars (admittedly at some remove, though the presence of war memorials on the island shows that it remained far from unscathed), the collapse of the fishing industry, significant changes in agriculture and forestry, major fluctuations in the tourist industry, the break-up of the Hamilton estate and the coming of the car ferry. This last, in particular, has caused huge changes in the lifestyle of the inhabitants of the island, not to mention in the nature of the inhabitants themselves.

The Tourist Merry-go-round

Arran at the turn of the century was still a semi-feudal playground for the titled and the *nouveaux riches,* and to some degree the estate was still run for the benefit of the field sports enthusiast rather than the local inhabitants. A number of circumstances have since combined to change the picture, although even at the present day there are occasional conflicts between tenant farmers and estate owners, concerning such matters as the fencing off of farm land to prevent the encroachment of deer.

The first factor contributing to the break-up of the Hamilton estate was the death of the 12th Duke of Hamilton in 1895. The estate passed to his daughter who, in 1906, married the

A submarine against the dramatic backdrop of Holy Isle formed the setting for the filming of a television advertisement aimed at persuading people throughout Britain that they cannot escape the need to buy a TV licence, no matter where they live!

Marquis of Graham (later to become the 6th Duke of Montrose). During the Montrose years, the island underwent many significant changes. Tourism expanded, partly due to the relaxation of restrictions on the taking in of paying guests by estate tenants and on the building of new houses, hotels and other facilities on the island. The island also was to benefit from the fundamental changes in the structure of society in general following the end of the First World War, in particular from the emancipation of the working classes and the spread of interest in outdoor relaxations among the middle classes.

Further changes were to follow after the death of the Duchess of Montrose in 1957, when death-duties forced the sale of Brodick Castle and its policies to the state, and the remainder of the estate was divided amongst various members of the family. Since then, large tracts of land have been sold to the Forestry Commission, the National Trust has been presented with Glen Rosa, Goatfell and surrounding areas

The *Waverley,* the last of the old paddle steamers still sailing the Firth of Clyde, in Brodick Bay. Summer cruises on this vessel have been very popular with holidaymakers over the years.

(some 7,000 acres in total) by Lady Jean Fforde, a daughter of the family who still retains the Strabane estate near Brodick, and other parts of the island have passed into private hands. With this fragmentation has come a relaxation of the estate's hold on tourist facilities, and Arran now has provision to match that of any of the other Scottish islands.

At the end of the First World War, the return of vast numbers of people from the trenches to work in the industrial towns of Clydeside and northern England, and the associated development of trade unions and the rise of the Labour Party, meant that there was a great increase in the numbers of people who had the means and the opportunity to take a holiday, even if only a day trip 'doon the Watter'. The aristocracy and the rich merchants still existed, but were now less significant factors in the economy of the Clyde coasts and islands. The demands of work, and the cost of living, meant that the summer-long renting of a holiday house was no longer a common practice. The decline in the use of servants meant that

Installing printing machinery at the Brodick offices of the *Arran Banner*, the local newspaper for the island. This journal is distributed to Arran lovers far and near, and is the best way to keep up with all that is happening on the island.

the problems of shopping and running a household on an island would have given the wife of the family little opportunity for rest and relaxation. Under these circumstances a two-month stay would have been closer to purgatory than heaven for some of the family!

The new mainstay of the island tourist industry were the middle classes, who developed a tradition over the years of the month's holiday, either staying in a hotel or boarding house, or renting a furnished house or cottage. At this time, steamers still called at many of the villages, and it was easy for visitors to reach their chosen holiday home almost no matter where on the island it was. Arran was still the preserve of the quiet family holiday, though. The mass tripper market looking for fun, after the style of Blackpool or Rothesay, has never had much interest in the island. Certainly, there were frequent day trips to the island, but often only as a port of call on a tour of the Firth of Clyde. It was only the east-coast pier villages — Brodick, Whiting Bay and Lamlash — that benefited much

The fish farm in Lamlash Bay, showing the pens in which the salmon are reared. The controversy aroused by this installation is centred on pollution of the bay by unused feedstuffs and chemicals given to the fish, together with worry about loss of amenity for the sailing and fishing fraternity based in the village of Lamlash, which can be seen spread out along the shore in the background.

from this trade, although Lochranza was a port of call for steamer trips to Campbeltown from Greenock or Gourock.

When trippers did land on Arran, the lack of 'facilities' did not encourage them to stay for very long. The most popular entertainment was a coach trip, usually around the island, stopping at a hotel for tea before the return to the tender mercy of the rolling boat deck on the homeward sail. Even in the late 1950s, after the advent of the first car ferries, caravans were not allowed on the island for fear that they might encourage the 'wrong type' of person to stay on the island instead of merely visiting it for a few hours! Whatever one may think of this attitude, it has done much to protect the island from the tawdry, faded glitz that now pervades some of the other resorts popular at that time.

The tripper industry on Arran would have been completely impracticable but for the great improvement in transport facilities that had taken place in the 1920s and '30s. As early as the 1920s there were a number of bus companies operating on Arran. Some of these only operated one route, usually linking Brodick and Lamlash to other parts of the island. There was even a Ford dealership established in Pirnmill before 1920, surely one of the least likely locations on Arran for such an enterprise! By the 1930s a network of bus routes meant that any visitor arriving at one of the piers could be sure of easy transport to guest house, hotel or rented cottage, no matter where it was. In this way the whole island became involved in the tourist trade, which was to displace agriculture as the mainstay of the island's economy.

Arran has, until the recent introduction of the car ferry from Lochranza to Claonaig in Kintyre, always been a place that visitors travelled to, rather than through. This has to some extent curtailed the level of what might be termed 'chance tourists', i.e., people using the island as a stepping-stone to the West Highlands, who just might require shelter and feeding overnight. In many parts of Scotland such visitors form a substantial part of the tourist trade, but it was not so in Arran until very recently. In some ways the absence of such a facility helped to keep the island the way the visitors liked it — rather exclusive.

If plans formulated in 1919 had come to fruition, Arran might have been a rather different place today. At that time a proposal was put forward for the building of a light railway between Blackwaterfoot and Whiting Bay, with possible later extension in the west to Machrie and Shiskine, and on the east to Lamlash and Brodick. This proposal came about as a result of a report, the Geddes Report of 1919, which investigated the state of rural transport systems in Scotland and suggested improvements and changes to the existing provisions. The intention behind the proposal was to form a link on a routeway between Islay and the Ayrshire coast. Passengers and goods would have been required to travel by ferry from Ardrossan to Whiting Bay. They would then have boarded the train to travel to Blackwaterfoot, transferred to a ferry to take them to Carradale in Kintyre, where a road service (using a route that was never built) would take them across the peninsula to the village of Tayinloan. At this point the weary travellers would again have taken to the water, in a ferry which the committee

The *Loch Ranza* was introduced on the Lochranza to Claonaig ferry service in 1987. It was specially designed to serve the route and has been a considerable success, greatly increasing the volume of both passenger and vehicle traffic crossing to and from Kintyre.

proposed should link Kintyre with Islay. At the time the only link in this complicated route which actually existed was the Ardrossan–Arran ferry. It was believed that the presence of a railway would stimulate trade and tourism in southern Arran in a way that the inadequate though rapidly expanding bus services would not be able to do.

In the event, delays in implementing the proposal allowed the road transport facilities to be improved to the point where no real benefit would have been gained from the construction of the line. It is tempting to speculate that the eventual abandonment of the idea deprived southern Arran of what might have become one of the major tourist attractions of the island, especially in the present era of enthusiasm for old steam trains.

Throughout the first half of the twentieth century, Arran retained and developed its image as a middle-class resort. The Official Guide Book produced by the Arran Publicity Association in the 1920s and 1930s contained many advertisements for hotels, guest houses and boarding houses, almost all of which took pains to highlight the proximity of the property to facilities such as golf, tennis, fishing, boating and bathing. The image (and the reality) of the island at that time was of a healthy, relaxing retreat from the stresses and strains of early twentieth-century life.

An attraction in those days before the First World War was the occasional presence of the Royal Navy. Both the Home and the Atlantic Fleets paid courtesy visits to the island, basing themselves in the great natural anchorage at Lamlash, as had the Viking fleet some 650 years earlier. When the Second World War broke out Lamlash again became a major centre of naval activity, and a gunnery school, landing craft training and a certain amount of ship repair were conducted in the bay behind the safety of entry booms at either end of Holy Isle. The author's mother could recall that at this time she still went to Arran as a summer visitor, so the tourist trade was not completely stifled by the conflict. At times, she said, there were so many ships anchored that she had the impression that you could have walked right across the bay by stepping from deck to deck.

After the war, Arran returned to its previous form of life, but a major change was to affect it in the mid-1950s. Before then, the only way vehicles could reach the island was as cargo, often deck cargo, on the steamers. Very few visitors took their cars with them to the island, preferring to rely on public transport or hired bicycles. Little wonder, when you realise that the only way to get them onto the ferries was to drive them up two planks from the quay to the deck, a hair-raising experience that probably caused quite a few drivers to look closely at their insurance policies!

As the motor car became increasingly popular, so pressure mounted to provide ferries designed to carry not only passengers, but their vehicles as well. The first car ferry, the *Arran*, came into service on the Ardrossan run in 1954, to be replaced in 1957 by the Glen Sannox, a much larger vessel. The changes that the advent of these vessels brought about were both rapid and profound.

The advent of the car-borne tourist was to deal a major blow to the small bus companies plying their trade around the roads

These boats are drawn up at the so-called 'Yellow Port' in Kildonan, used by commercial traffic as recently as 1946, but now the haunt only of small dinghies.

of the island. Many of them were too small to continue supporting routes that could not generate enough traffic to be profitable, and gradually they disappeared through a combination of merger with larger companies and the closure of uneconomic routes. In 1973 the Arran Transport and Trading Company came into being, acting both as a haulage and transport company serving the island and as the umbrella organisation for Arran Coaches, which now has a monopoly of the local bus trade. The services supported by the company are a valuable contribution to island life, helping to link outlying parts of the island with such central facilities as the pier at Brodick and the High School at Lamlash, of which more anon. In addition to the scheduled services, the company also runs coach tours of the island in the summer, particularly for day visitors, though with the introduction in 1984 of the *Isle of Arran*, a vehicle ferry with greatly increased capacity over its predecessors, more coach tours from the mainland bring the bus and passengers across to stay on the island for a couple of nights or so before moving on to their next destination.

Public transport of a slightly different type is available on the island in the form of Postbus services. These serve a number of the smaller settlements, but the demand for them is quite low, and the provision for passengers is gradually being reduced.

The coming of the car ferry proved to be the final nail in the coffin as far as most of the piers on Arran were concerned. Even before this date, the condition of the piers at Whiting Bay and Lamlash had been deteriorating, while Brodick pier had to be given a concrete surface to make it safe for vehicles coming on and off the ferry. It was clear that the amount of traffic coming to the island did not justify the upgrading of any more than the one pier. Although there were still sailings to Arran by steamers which carried only passengers, Lamlash pier was closed in 1954 and Whiting Bay pier closed in 1957. In this same year, the steamer link from Lochranza to Campbeltown ceased operation, and although Lochranza pier was never officially closed it was not used again except for mooring the occasional fishing boat. It has been sadly allowed to fall into such a state of neglect that storm damage has reduced it to a twisted heap of planks.

With the closure of the other piers, Brodick achieved a pre-eminent position on the island. As virtually all goods and visitors had to land there, it is hardly surprising that the village rapidly became the commercial centre for the island. A few small boats still used the tiny harbour at Blackwaterfoot, and the pier at Lochranza, but these anchorages increasingly became the haunt of inshore fishing dinghies and holiday boats. With the introduction of roll-on/roll-off ferries in 1970, a special ramp was constructed at Brodick to serve these boats. The biggest advantage of this change was the greatly increased speed of loading and emptying the boats, but the disadvantage which soon came to light was that if Ardrossan were stormbound (as happens not infrequently during the winter), the nearest sheltered roll-on/roll-off landing facilities on the mainland side were at Gourock, a diversion which more than doubled the crossing time and could create havoc with timetables, not to mention the inconvenience suffered by the poor souls who got tossed around on the stormy sea for some two and a half hours and were often then deposited on the mainland at a strange port. However, this problem affects mainly the islanders themselves and those hardy souls who are besotted enough to visit the island at all times of year!

An exciting goalmouth incident in the 1988 Arran Cup Final between Brodick and Lamlash. Half a dozen sides contest a local league as well as the cup each year — providing yet another focal point for friendly inter-community rivalry on the island.

In an attempt to generate further tourist traffic on Arran, a new car ferry linking Lochranza with Claonaig in Kintyre was started in 1972, using a landing-craft type of vessel which disembarked cars and passengers at a concrete slipway just beside the old pier. This service, which runs only in summer, has proved to be very popular — so much so that a much larger 'landing craft' the *Lochranza*, started on the run in April 1987. The increased capacity of this vessel has been justified by further growth in traffic, although the hoped-for advent of coach tours using Arran as a stepping-stone to the west coast and the Hebrides has still not materialised. In part, this is due to the road on the Claonaig side being so narrow and twisty that it is difficult for a car to drive at any speed, never mind a bus. If the promised upgrade of the Claonaig Road ever does come about, then it is quite likely that further benefit will accrue to Arran.

The ease with which the visitor can take a car to Arran has produced more adjustments in the type of holiday provision on the island. When people came on foot, using the local bus service to transfer them from the boat, they travelled relatively lightly. Clothes, golf clubs, tennis rackets and possibly fishing rods were quite enough to carry without bringing along household utensils, food etc. Thus the hotels and boarding houses did good business, providing all the creature comforts that the guest might require, and letting houses were popular only with the wealthy or the family groups who could disperse the loads to be carried around a large number of people. The coming of the car changed things greatly. It was now possible to carry linen, towels, food and other essentials of civilised living, as well as clothes and sports equipment and, what is more, to take them with ease to virtually any address on the island. The letting house, usually rented for the fortnight or the month, became very much more popular. Local shops and supermarkets have sprung up in several villages in recent years to cater for the boom in demand for foodstuffs etc. from self-catering holidaymakers.

In 1968, letting-house accommodation was nearly double that of hotels, but this figure began to change in the 1970s. At this time hotel accommodation was still increasing slightly, but the letting facilities began to decline partly as a result of the buying-up of such properties as second homes, often by those very holidaymakers who had previously rented them. This decline was to some extent offset by the introduction of camping and caravan facilities, albeit on a somewhat restricted scale. It is somewhat ironic that the introduction of such facilities was long resisted, as it was feared that they might attract a 'less desirable' class of visitor, but by the 1970s was contributing quite significantly to the very survival of the island's tourist economy.

The actual setting up of formal designated camp sites was in fact a somewhat belated acceptance of a situation that had been in existence for some time. In summer, large numbers of young people come to the island looking for somewhere to pitch a tent, and eventually it was recognised that if this was going to happen anyway, it would be better to have some control as to where it happened. It is one of the facts of Arran life that there is relatively little low-cost accommodation on the island. There are two Youth Hostels, at Whiting Bay and at Lochranza, and a few other outlets such as small cheap chalet

Swimming gala at the swimming pool in Blackwaterfoot.

developments, but nothing on a scale large enough to cater for the thousands who come to Arran in July and August and for the infamous holiday weekends, and who neither could, nor would, wish to pay the going rates for a letting-house or guesthouse accommodation. Much as some residents of the island would like it to remain a middle-class playground, camping and caravanning facilities bring large numbers of people who would not otherwise come. They spend large amounts of money in the shops and pubs (not necessarily in that order) and make a significant contribution to the wealth of the island.

Since the 1970s, there have been further changes in the structure of the holiday business on Arran. In 1988, the number of hotel beds available had fallen, and self-catering facilities had again increased in number. In part this is due to the influence of competition from cheap overseas package holidays with guaranteed sunshine, in part due to the increasing importance in the Scottish tourist industry as a whole, of coach-based parties — a trade Arran largely misses out on — and in part due to a change in the habits of the middle-class visitors who are still the mainstay of the tourist industry. The popular taste has again moved towards the extra freedom and flexibility offered by self-catering facilities and away from the slightly rigid (and rather more expensive) régime of the hotel, aided to some extent by an increase in the number of restaurants and bars in which it is possible to buy a reasonable meal and thereby lighten the drudgery of domestic chores.

The increase in self-catering facilities has been produced partly by the spread of chalet facilities. These buildings, usually wooden and of Scandinavian design, might not be thought to blend well with the heather moors and mountains typical of the west coast of Scotland, but with the spread of forestry across much of Arran, the entire scene is becoming more and more Scandinavian and the chalets often blend in quite well, though the effect is sometimes spoilt by having them clustered too closely together rather like a site full of wooden caravans.

The visitor might also be struck by the amount of building work that some hotels have embarked on and think that they were upgrading in an attempt to recapture their former importance for the tourist industry. To some extent that is true, but some of this work actually marks the end of the traditional hotel industry. The fluctuations have brought some hotels to the point of insolvency, while others are attempting to stave off the evil day by changing their function. At present there is a minor trend towards the adapting of hotel buildings for other purposes. Some are being converted into self-catering apartments, while the Whiting Bay Hotel was sold in 1987 and converted into a home for the elderly.

The Population See-saw

The popularity of the island with the visitor seems still to be quite healthy. In 1987, Brodick Castle recorded over 60,000 visitors, which put it among the top ten National Trust properties in Scotland. The number of tourists seeking accommodation on the island at times in July and August is such that the Tourist Board has to seek out locals who do not normally take in visitors and ask them to put people up for a

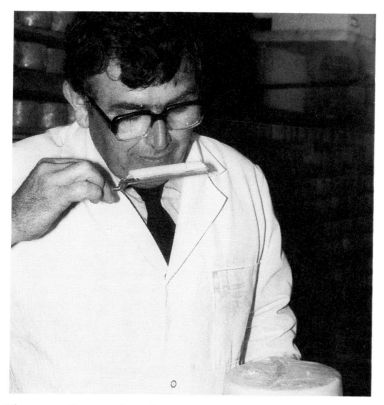

The state of maturation of an Arran cheese being checked at the creamery at Torrylinn. Cheeses from the island are exported all over the world.

night or two. This all helps to give the impression that Arran is a boom area, but what is it really like in the winter, when visitors are a tiny minority and the 'real' life of the island can proceed unhindered?

The quality of life for the Arranach has changed considerably over the course of the last eighty years, and these changes can be mirrored in the changes in population during this period. In 1901, the population according to the census was 4,766. The numbers were to remain steady until after the 1951 census, which showed that at that time there were still over 4,600 souls in permanent residence. The 1961 census created great alarm, however, as it showed a population of only 3,577, a 20 per cent decline in a decade, which prompted the Isle of Arran Council of Social Service to commission a report on the future population trends which might be expected. This report, written by Margaret Storrie and C.I. Jackson, analysed the reasons behind the population decline and estimated that if nothing were done, by 1981 the population could be as low as 2,000! They also suggested ways in which this decline might be halted or at least slowed down. The report was in fact published in 1967, by which time the population had dropped to about 3,300 people, seeming to bear out Storrie and Jackson's worst fears.

What produced this catastrophic decline in population? A number of causes have been suggested in various reports, all of which highlighted the difficulties of finding permanent employment on Arran. The chief villains of the piece were the motor vehicle and electricity, both of which made life easier for the inhabitants, but which greatly reduced labour requirements. By 1965, only 31 per cent of the adult male population were employed in agriculture, a figure which dropped to 23 per cent by 1971. Many of those who lost their jobs would have looked to switch to work in the holiday industry, but the seasonality of employment, together with the fact that here too there was contraction of employment, meant that it offered very little hope for those with families to feed. The natural result was emigration, both to the mainland cities and, sometimes, to the Antipodes or to the Americas.

The majority of those who left Arran at this time were young men and their families, with a sprinkling of the middle-aged as well. Most of them had already known a world beyond the island, as all Arran children had to go to school outside the island, at least for senior secondary education. Until 1955, they had to go to Ardrossan, by courtesy of an arrangement between Bute and Ayrshire county councils. After 1955, they had to go to Rothesay for any form of senior secondary education, a consequence of the building of a larger and more modern school after the old Ardrossan Academy building was destroyed by fire in 1955. Thus from the age of twelve, the brightest children on the island effectively were boarded out to school, in the process losing contact with much of Arran life

Vintage car enthusiasts often use Arran as the base for rallies and other gatherings, especially in summer.

and developing new friends and interests which were difficult to maintain on Arran. It was precisely these people whom island society could least afford to lose, and yet they proved to be the most vulnerable to the blandishments of the mainland.

The loss of population was a problem which was not to be easily remedied, according to the Storrie report. It was thought that agriculture was likely to increase in output, but that the amalgamation of farms would make it more efficient and further reduce the need for farm labour. Tourism was a seasonal source of work, but most of the labour needed by the hotels, guest houses etc. was provided by students and others looking for temporary work. Industry was not thought a likely solution, as the island was both deficient in raw materials and was remote from any market in which to sell products. The main hope seemed to be to encourage retired people to buy property on Arran and to come to live there. These people need shops for food, clothes and other staples of life, and they need them all year round. Shops would thus have an elevated level of trade in winter, and there would be jobs also in service industries such as plumbing, decorating and building.

The next census count showed a minor rise in population, and by the 1980s the population was over 4,000 and reasonably stable. As predicted, the number of people retiring to the island was to increase, and a number of the younger Arranachs now stay on as tradesmen to provide services for them. Local builders have prospered over the past twenty years, and new bungalows and small estates have sprung up on the outskirts of several of the villages. Many of these properties have been bought by elderly incomers, happy to settle into a new house in a beautiful and peaceful environment. Many of them had long and happy associations with the island before they retired, and have generally settled easily into the local way of life.

Another factor which helped the population recovery was the raising, in the 1970s, of the status of Arran High School to provide senior secondary educational facilities. This decision, the fruit of a long campaign, means that nowadays Arran children can continue their education on the island, right up to university entrance level. This has helped to keep young people on the island, and, together with the greater employment prospects which the advent of the retirement 'industry' brought, and some other business initiatives recently started on the island, has created a more optimistic atmosphere about the future of Arran.

A third element of the present population is rather more difficult to assess. These are the so-called 'white settlers', usually English, who have come to the island in the last decade or two looking to escape from the city rat-race. They may have been to the island on holiday, liked what they saw, and decided to try and make a living there, forgetting sometimes that winter in Arran is a far cry from the idylls of summer.

There have been two waves of 'white settler' invasion. The earlier of these probably peaked in the early 1970s, and consisted largely of people trying to get back to a simpler life-style without the stresses and strains of high commerce, motorway traffic jams and supermarket queues. At this time there were a lot of old crofts and farm cottages lying empty and abandoned on the island. The incomers often bought them, restored them, and set up craft workshops producing

Golf is one of the many facilities available to both local and visitor on Arran. In all there are seven courses on the island, each with its own character. Here a group tee off on Brodick golf course.

such items as jewellery, candles, pottery, wood carvings and paintings, which they sold to the summer tourists. Arran had long been attractive to artists, some of whom came to live on the island. The new arrivals were simply reflecting this pattern, but on an amplified scale. Probably the main centre to which the 'crafts-people' came was Whiting Bay, where there is still what is probably the highest concentration in the island of such cottage industries, but most of the villages now can boast at least one resident craftsman of some description. Some, such as the sculptor Alasdair Dunn who died recently, established a reputation far beyond the confines of the island. Others were content simply to make a living in their own individual way, secure in their island 'fortress'.

The second wave is of a rather different nature. Unlike the crafts-people, who were generally of an age to have a young family when they moved to Arran, the second group are rather older, often of an age when the children have just left home and they are no longer tied by considerations of schooling. The route by which this group comes to Arran is by taking over an established small business, such as a guest house or shop. Many of these incomers again are English, often from Yorkshire. Indeed so many of them have now settled in the south-east of the island that the Whiting Bay area is sometimes jokingly referred to as 'Little Yorkshire'. Although many of these incomers settle in well, the business does not always turn out as expected and they may stay for only a few years before moving on. Because they merely take over a business rather than founding one, often there is no increase in population because the previous owners of the business leave the island.

The coming of the 'white settlers' has provided some problems for the community to solve. Because many of them have come to escape, they are often reluctant to see their rural retreat developed. Many are environmentally concerned, and form pressure groups to try and resist changes they may believe to be harmful to the quality of their way of life. Sometimes these concerns run counter to those of the native islanders who may favour the development because it will provide jobs, and they are not interested in the 'fossilisation' of Arran as a living museum of the mid-twentieth century. The native Arranach is somewhat reticent by nature, and it is often

Fresh fruit, vegetables and other provisions being landed at Brodick from a small vessel which brought them from the mainland during a ferry strike which isolated the island for 10 days in March 1988.

the incomers who put themselves forward for positions of responsibility in the community. This has led to the suggestion that at times the Arran people are not in control of their own lives, a suggestion which has sometimes produced a degree of resentment. At least one incoming hotelier left the island recently after complaining about a 'whispering campaign' against him.

There is a danger that if Arran continues to attract incomers and retired people as it has over the past twenty years, the Arranach will become a minority in his own island. Already the population has reached the point where there is pressure on housing facilities, and few of the local people can compete with the incomers when it comes to offering for a house coming on the market. This is not so bad if the buyer is coming to the island to live, but if it is to be used as a second home, occupied for only a month or two each year, then resentment may arise. Some of the smaller Arran clachans are virtually ghost villages for much of the year because of this trade in holiday houses. If this trend is allowed to run unchecked, then it is quite possible that the spectre of depopulation will raise its head again.

Local Industry and Employment Opportunities

Over the years, the staples of Arran employment have been agriculture and tourism. Fishing has declined to the point almost of extinction, save for some lobster and crab fishing. At the beginning of this century, fishing boats operated out of Lochranza and Pirnmill and caught herring in the waters of the Clyde, but the use of larger boats and the growth of centralised market facilities on the mainland meant that the small island fisheries could no longer compete. Arran men still found work as fishers, but this meant working on boats based in Ayr or Tarbert or some other port. The trend was for fishermen either to leave their trade or to leave the island.

In the 1980s, a revival in fishing and fish processing has provided a few jobs on the island. A fish farm has been started in Lamlash Bay, and is currently rearing some 150,000 salmon, while a smokehouse has been operating in Lamlash, producing delicacies both for local consumption and for export to the mainland. Permission has recently been granted to the owners, Marine Harvest, for a major expansion of the fishfarm area. Although the cages are in a remote part of Lamlash Bay, and are not visible from the main tourist routes, there are local worries about potential pollution of the bay, and about the level of stress liable to result from increased traffic on the access road.

Agriculture has also changed considerably during the course of the twentieth century, and its importance as a source of jobs for Arran men has declined enormously in the past eighty-odd years. The impression of the land as seen from the ferry when it enters Brodick Bay and nears the pier is almost the same as it would have been fifty years ago — the towering hills and the Castle policies to the north, and, on the lower slopes to the south, green pasture divided into fields by verdant hedgerows. The keen student of Arran history would notice the differences most in the character of the higher slopes on the south side of the bay, where a dark blanket of trees now covers what once was heather moorland. The planting of trees by the Forestry Commission has produced a major impact on many aspects of Arran life, not all of them seen as beneficial by the inhabitants.

The first plantations by the Forestry Commission on the

Auchrannie, a large house just outside Brodick, is the location for the first timeshare development on the island, combining sports and hotel facilities with luxurious apartments. This may be a pointer to the direction which the tourist industry on Arran may have to follow if it is to match competition from elsewhere in Britain, not to mention abroad.

island took place in 1952, when an area on the Glenrickard estate, on the slopes around Glen Cloy was planted. Since then, they have acquired large tracts of land on the island, and substantial parts of the southern end have fallen beneath a green cloak. The extent of afforestation has been increased by some private planting as well, and trees are now growing on some of the moorland areas fringing the northern hills, as well as in the southern half. Almost a third of the total area of the island is either under trees already or is being considered for planting, a situation which has drawn objections from bodies such as the Nature Conservancy Council, worried about the loss of important geological sites beneath the bough as well as the plough.

The number of jobs provided by forestry work has varied. In 1963, during one of the major phases of planting, the number employed was twenty-eight. Ten years later the number had fallen to ten, partly because the use of power tools and improved technology meant fewer men were needed, but also because the labour requirements dropped once the level of planting declined. If needed, seasonal labour is engaged to supplement the resident workers.

The first timber felled for export to the mainland was taken off the island in 1987. It is hoped that the felling of trees will become a steady source of employment, particularly if the giant new papermill that is scheduled to start work in Irvine takes Arran timber. The first loads are being cut from the trees near the top of the Brodick–Lamlash road. Felling in this area serves a dual purpose, as not only is the timber handy for the pier at Brodick, but the trees that are being cut were often accused of blocking one of the finest views on Arran. Many residents had objected to afforestation quite vehemently on the grounds that it would spoil those aspects of the island which most attracted tourists, and tourism supported many more livelihoods than forestry did. The drab colour of the early plantings, and the screening of the roads as the trees grew up, did indeed give some regions an atmosphere rather more like parts of the Black Forest than a Scottish island!

In fairness, it has to be said that some attempt has been made by the Forestry Commission to vary the species planted so as to give more colour to the landscape, and they have also instigated a policy of felling or thinning trees close to viewpoints. In addition, the provision of forest walkways and picnic areas has generally benefited the tourist industry on the island. Whether in general the impact of such large-scale planting is for the better or not is a matter of personal taste, but again it is a small-scale reflection of events happening across Scotland as a whole.

Other changes have taken place in Arran agriculture. The predominance of milk cattle grazed on the lowland pastures has given way to a considerable extent to the raising of beasts for beef production, and the traditional breeds such as Ayrshires are now seen at the Arran Agricultural Show in the company of relatively recent incomers such as Charolais. For a time in the mid-1980s the numbers of cattle being offered for sale at the Brodick market were so low as to threaten the viability of the event, but since then things have improved.

The Brodick Highland Games, held every August, attract large crowds to watch displays and traditional athletic events such as hammer throwing and tossing the caber.

Dairying is far from extinct. Arran Dairies at Brodick have a thriving trade, collecting, pasteurising and packing milk for sale to the island, as well as shipping some to the creamery at Torrylinn. The creamery, started in the 1950s, makes a Dunlop-style cheese of award-winning quality, much of which is sold abroad — to the consternation of the hapless holidaymaker who may at times have difficulty buying it on the

The most successful business on the island, Arran Provisions have had to expand into this new factory in Lamlash in order to keep up with the demand for their products.

island where it is produced! This problem was not helped by a reduction in the level of output, due in part to a drop in milk supply as farmers switched to beef from dairying. In May 1987 an increase in the milk quota seemed to have saved the creamery from possible closure, and at the time of writing its future seems secure.

The most stable element of the farming picture on the island has been sheep production, though the grazing has become increasingly directed towards pasture as hill grazings have disappeared beneath trees. The sheep are usually sold to the mainland for fattening off for slaughter, though local lambs were sometimes sold directly for butchering. The export of lambs was almost totally disrupted by the effects of radioactive fallout following the Chernobyl nuclear disaster in April 1986. Arran was one of the areas in which restrictions on the movement and sale of sheep were imposed, causing acute problems for some farmers for the following two or three years.

The keeping of poultry on the island is quite widespread, but even the larger producers still sell only to the local market. It is simply not worthwhile taking the products to the mainland for

The tiny harbour at Blackwaterfoot may see a new lease of life if a proposal to inaugurate a small ferry to Campbeltown in Kintyre ever comes to fruition.

sale. No longer produced for export either are the famous Arran potatoes, which used to be grown on the light sandy soils fringing the coast. In the first half of the century this was a thriving trade, led by the 'Potato King', Donald McKelvie of Lamlash, who produced over thirty new varieties of potato, now grown the world over. He ceased his work in 1947, and since then the local potato industry has declined to the point where Arran-grown potatoes are almost exclusively for local consumption.

The mild climate of Arran has attracted some people to grow early vegetables, flowers and herbs for sale to the mainland, though as yet this is hardly on a scale where it could be called an industry. The use of local produce by the increasing number of quality eating houses, both restaurants and hotels, on the island has become more noticeable over the past few years, and may be seen as a pointer to the future of Arran agriculture.

As specialist and quality foodstuffs are increasingly being produced, so local industries have begun to spring up and take advantage of these raw materials. We have already mentioned the creamery and the fish smoking plant, but other, larger,

Lochranza Castle, built on a gravel spit, guards the entrance to the anchorage of Loch Ranza. This is the area that would be most affected if the recent proposal to build a marina in the village were ever to be realised.

stirrings are abroad on the island. Despite the failure only a few years ago of one enterprise in Brodick which produced such goodies as venison pâté and marmalade with whisky, food processing is going from strength to strength. Arran Provisions, which started out making exotic varieties of mustard, gradually built up a trade which resulted in their being taken over by the major food producers, Robertson and Baxter, in 1986. Since then the company has gone from strength to strength, culminating in the construction of a purpose-built new factory opposite the old meal mill site at the foot of the Ross Road. They are now probably the largest single enterprise on the island, maintaining a workforce of fifty even in low season, rising to over seventy during busy periods. As the range of products has expanded to bring in jams, jellies and preserves, so the sales returns have also expanded, the company having a turnover in 1988 of over £2 million from worldwide outlets.

In a similar vein, a company producing a range of soaps, shampoos and other perfumed objects has recently started near Brodick, while other small cottage industries are also

In the summer months, the level of traffic on the island roads can give rise to problems of parking and free flow of vehicles. Here in Brodick the difficulties reached such a level in the mid-1980s that parking restrictions had to be introduced, a revolutionary move that produced a lot of adverse reaction from local inhabitants.

producing goods aimed at the luxury market on the mainland. It remains to be seen whether there is room for all these enterprises in the island economy, but the signs are hopeful in that at least the island is forward-looking rather than slumped in pessimism and apathy.

Unfortunately there are some developments and initiatives which are seen as ill-founded or even harmful by much of the local population. The most notorious of these is the Brodick beach sand 'scandal'. In the 1970s concern began to be expressed about the consequences of the extraction of sand from the mouth of the Rosa Burn. It was being washed and graded, and then sold for use as a filtration medium for water supplies in places such as Saudi Arabia. Permission was originally granted on the basis of established practice, but soon Arran Estates were asking for a quadrupling of the extraction rate, and Cunninghame District Council issued the necessary permissions. At about the same time, a vociferous local action group started to try to get the permission revoked, on the grounds that the extraction of the sand was causing erosion of the coast around the bay, and the beach sand was becoming coarser and less attractive to tourists as a result.

A similar fate had befallen Catacol beach in the 1920s and 1930s, when sand and gravel was exported for use in the building of the Loch Sloy hydro-electric scheme. This resulted in the loss of a safe channel in which the locals used to draw up their boats. In the case of Brodick, the effects are still ongoing. The erosion of the beach has resulted in the local putting green losing some land to the sea, and in a potential threat to parts of the golf course. The extractors and the local authority contend that this is just a natural process which would have occurred anyway, but the coincidence with the onset of large-scale extraction from the beach is too great for that argument to be accepted by most of the local people, especially those who feel the tourist industry will suffer as a result of this loss of amenity. The argument still goes on, and while it does, the extraction and the erosion continue, most notably along the beach to the north of the mouth of the Rosa.

Modern Arran – Paradise or Purgatory?

At present Arran is looking a lot healthier socially and economically than it was feared it would as recently as twenty years ago. From the beginning of the century, the population fell steadily if slowly, and it was not until the coming of the 'retirement trade' and the 'white settlers' that the trend was reversed, as we have seen. For many of these people, the move to Arran was an attempt at finding their own special paradise, a quiet non-industrial island of enormous natural beauty being the attraction. For many of them, the dream became reality only for a while, and then the hardships of island life began to chip away at their idealised picture. Is it reasonable to say that they have ended up committing themselves to purgatory?

Modern Arran life is of a remarkably high quality compared with that on many other offshore islands in Britain. There are excellent social service facilities with health visitors and district nurses who can visit the elderly or bedridden, a very well equipped hospital in Lamlash where, so it is said, they can perform operations up to about the level of a kidney transplant, though anything more serious has to go to the mainland for treatment. To assist in the rapid evacuation of the patient a helicopter landing pad has been constructed at the hospital. The island is also well supplied with doctors, so the settlers need have little fear of landing themselves in a medical desert. Whether that level of care can be maintained if more hotels are converted into private nursing homes and the proportion of elderly people in the island population increases remains to be seen.

For the fitter and slightly wealthier, one of the signs of the new prosperity in Arran society is the fact that some of the better hotels and restaurants now stay open through the winter as well as in the tourist season. It is possible to dine out in real quality in Arran every day of the year, should the finances be up to the strain — a far cry from the picture not so long ago when everything on the island closed after the September weekend, and only reopened at Easter.

A less happy side of island life can be seen in the prices of goods in the shops. Arran is undoubtedly a very expensive place in which to buy many of the staples of life. Bread is baked in Brodick, but most other groceries and commonplace household goods have to come across on the ferry. This adds to their price, and the local cost of living may come as a rude shock to the city escapee used to having a choice of supermarkets. The problem becomes even more acute with regard to items such as clothing, where naturally the range stocked locally is somewhat limited. The only real choice is often either to use a mail order catalogue (though not all companies will send goods to an offshore island) or to go on the ferry to somewhere like Irvine or Glasgow.

The disillusionment that can set in after a while is in most cases only temporary, but it cannot be denied that every year a few incomers decide to move on to new pastures. Let us hope, however, that Arran retains its island privations, for without them it may become like the places from which the incomers were escaping in the first place. It is those very aspects of life that made it purgatory for the few that have kept it paradise for the great majority, and long may that remain so!

CHAPTER 10

The Future of Arran

As the title of this chapter implies, it is time for a little conjecture. The problems facing Arran are many and varied, and the way in which the island will evolve in future depends on the solutions adopted to overcome these difficulties. In particular, will the native Arranach become an endangered species? It is all very well saying that the unique attraction of the island is its peace and tranquillity amid glorious scenery, but the person who says that is missing out on one of the essentials of the Celtic view of the world, that the land and the people who live on it are indivisable, linked by emotional bonds so strong that they rival or even surpass ties between members of a family. Arran without the Arranach is not Arran at all, but instead some pretty wallpaper decorating otherwise empty and meaningless lives.

The Arran native is already familiar from long experience with the effects of hordes of people, strangers for the most part, swamping the locals for much of the summer. This does not mean to say that the island community does not exist at that time, but in some ways it goes 'underground', only emerging in full when the hubbub and clamour of the summer have died down. One has only to look at the pages of the *Arran Banner,* the local weekly newspaper notable, among other things, for having the highest market penetration of any equivalent publication in Britain, to see the number of social events and clubs that function in the dull dark months of winter. The problem is that as the proportion of incomers increases in the population, so it may be that the native-born people feel aliens in their own backyards, and the social fabric begins to disintegrate.

In practice, the problem is less acute than it might be. Most of the incomers make a real effort to integrate and, providing they don't push too hard, are eventually accepted although the difference is never forgotten. The major areas of potential conflict are development and modernisation of facilities on the island: the native is pleased to see changes that may make life easier or may provide employment, and is less worried about changes to the environment than the incomer anxious to preserve the island the way it was. Those people who would try to keep Arran as a sort of living museum have a certain similarity of attitude to those Dukes of Hamilton who wanted to keep the peasantry from hunting the deer and generally tried to maintain the island as a game reserve for themselves and their friends to hunt in to their hearts' content. Arran must be allowed to breathe, to develop, if it is to maintain its soul. If the people feel compelled to leave and seek a better lifestyle on the mainland, then gradually that soul will be lost, and all that makes up the magic of the island will go with it.

Employment is the basic problem. If it is plentiful, then the island will flourish. If it withers and dies, then the island community will be abandoned to the creeping decay of suburban attitudes and lifestyles. One of the keys to the direction in which the island will go is transport. Arran is almost unique among the larger Scottish islands in not possessing an airfield. In the 1930s there was a grass strip near Shiskine, and flights from Glasgow to Campbeltown would stop there on request. Since those days, the only air links with the mainland have been emergency helicopter trips ferrying patients from the hospital at Lamlash. An attempt was made in 1984 to establish a helicopter mail service between Brodick and Ardrossan. After a trial period the idea was abandoned, largely due to difficulties in finding a suitable landing site at Ardrossan. More recently, the idea of building a grass strip for small aircraft at Drumadoon has been raised and is currently being investigated. The problem is that the proposed strip is very close to, or may even cross, some major archaeological sites. If permission is given for this development, it is quite possible that further skirmishes between the preservationists and the rest could develop.

If Arran is not to be at a permanent economic disadvantage because of its isolation from the market place, some changes will have to come about with respect to the ferry services — the present island lifeline, and unlikely to change that function in the foreseeable future. For a long time, various island bodies in Scotland have been lobbying for the imposition of a Road Equivalent Tariff on ferries, modelled on the Norwegian system. Such a system would greatly cut the cost of transport to and from the island, and at a stroke would alter the economics of manufacturing industries on Arran. Island-produced goods would then be better able to compete in the market place with those made elsewhere. The cost of living on the island, currently one of the highest in Britain in respect of such vital commodities as petrol, would be reduced to levels very like those on the mainland. Although it is doubtful that hordes of industrialists would come flocking to Arran under such circumstances, some small companies might be encouraged to set up there.

The possible future sketched out in the preceding paragraph might not appeal to everyone on the island. The true Arranach is likely to welcome a drop in the cost of living, and welcome very much an increased employment opportunity. If this came about, many people who currently leave the island in search of better-paid work on the mainland might be encouraged to remain. This would result in population growth which, when put together with the anticipated increase in commercial activity, would put pressure on building land. Those who retired to Arran in search of its unique combination of peace and beauty might feel moved to object to such developments which could be seen as threatening the character of the island. This is already the case at Lamlash, where a public meeting held in January 1989 to discuss the implications of a proposed expansion of the fish farm in the Bay showed that such issues clearly divided the community. One group were vehemently opposed to the development on environmental grounds, including the effect of heavy lorries on narrow island roads, while another group could think of the proposal only in terms of an employment opportunity which was to be welcomed.

The coming of an employment boom to Arran in the wake of the introduction of a Road Equivalent Tariff is only a pipe-dream, of course. Alas, rather darker prophesies look to have more substance to them. The Government has been investigating the possibility of privatising ferry services in Scotland. Although the present threat to the Ardrossan-Brodick link has abated, the discussion associated with the proposal indicated some of the difficulties that might ensue were the idea ever to be implemented. In private hands, the first responsibility of any company managing the service would be to maximise the return to their shareholders, in other words to raise profits as much as possible. Whatever may be said about the present Caledonian MacBrayne service, they do schedule regular crossings all year round, even at times when they know they will carry only a handful of passengers and a couple of vehicles. In essence, they are a vital lifeline, carrying goods and people to and from the island. In private hands, it is difficult to see sailings that inevitably run at a loss being maintained on the schedule. In winter, particularly, one might anticipate a further reduction in sailings, possibly even to the frequency of some of the present-day routes to the Outer Hebrides which run maybe two or three times per week. At the same time it is possible that, even for the summer boom, fares might have to be raised significantly just to maintain a profit margin.

Such a scenario is not one to be welcomed on Arran. When the threat of privatisation was first raised, the local reaction was that it would hurt business, probably raise the cost of living, and make the island a much less attractive place in which to make a home. There were even tales of the mainland terminus of the route being shifted to the safer, but more distant, harbour of Troon. Such a change would increase the journey time by something like twenty minutes, make the ferry more expensive to run, and almost certainly produce further rises in fares. In order to protect the interest of islanders, a local group was formed on Arran, Cumbrae and Bute when privatisation was first mentioned, with a view to bidding for the Clyde routes and then employing a management team to run the services. Thankfully, the necessity for such a move has now receded, for the meantime at least.

The tourist industry, likely to be the largest single factor in the future economy, just as it has been for the past century, will have to adapt to changing circumstances. Arran must maintain and expand tourist provision, offering the holidaymaker incentives to come to the island which are strong enough to overcome any resistance produced by the cost of the ferry crossing. The island tourist board already does a great deal, sending information about Arran and its attractions to enquirers all over the world, and helping those who have arrived on the island to find accommodation or to locate particular facilities. To some degree the numbers of visitors are rising again, after the drastic decline in numbers caused by the British population discovering that Europe offered rather more than Ayr or Clacton in the way of sun and sand. To keep the visitors interested, places like Arran have to offer something to compensate for the relatively poor climate when compared with the Mediterranean or Turkey. Beauty is all very well, but is it enough for the tourist of the future?

The island needs both places for visitors to stay and things for them to do. Some of the larger hotels are currently being converted into self-catering apartments, a reflection of one change in current tastes. There is still a need for good hotels, though, and the injection of large sums of cash may be required to bring many of them up to the standard today's visitors now expect. One hotel in Brodick is currently launching into the timeshare apartment market, offering weeks for sale in luxury accommodation which can be yours or your descendants' in perpetuity. Such weeks can also be traded against other similar weeks in timeshares all over the globe. One advantage of this scheme is that it may bring visitors from other countries who would never otherwise have seen Arran. If the island can make itself sufficiently alluring in their eyes, then they may be back in future, and they will certainly spread the word about the glories of Arran among their friends in New York, Copenhagen or Munich. The future of Arran tourism may be a much more international one than previously.

However good the accommodation may be, the island will have only a limited attraction for tourists if there is nothing to occupy them in the evenings, or during wet weather. In an attempt to offset such problems, and at the same time lengthen the visitor season, an increasing number of 'activity holidays' are beginning to appear on the Arran tourist register. Pony-trekking is one such activity already well-established, while residential courses, including tuition and board, can now be had in such topics as handicrafts, natural history and golf. Field centres offering board, tuition and local expertise for school, college and university parties have opened in Lochranza and Shiskine, while many of the hotels extend their season by catering for similar parties (usually of geologists) at Easter and in the autumn. Activities could be extended to include water sports, painting, weaving, jewellery making, walking, music making etc. — many of which are independent of weather and could operate successfully at almost any time of year. With the increase in leisure time available to many people and the increasing proportion of retired people in the population, such holidays could prove an invaluable boost to the island economy.

Some more grandiose schemes for the future development of tourist provision on Arran have surfaced in the late 1980s, though how many of them will ever materialise remains to be seen. For example, a proposal for the construction of a marina at Lochranza with berthing facilities for 300 boats was reported in the *Arran Banner* in February 1987, raising some protests from the locals who thought such a development would completely swamp the village. To the relief of some, and the disappointment of others, nothing more has been heard of the scheme. As the waters of the Firth of Clyde are such a good boating area, and Arran is a very convenient centre from which to explore the sea lochs and more open waters, it is unlikely that this will be the last such scheme to be put to the planners.

One particular spectre haunts the tourist industry, not just in Arran but almost throughout the seaside resorts in Britain, and that is the growth in provision of residential homes for the elderly. The conversion of many hotels for that purpose would remove vital facilities for the summer visitor. In addition to Montrose House, the recently-built regional home for the elderly in Brodick, a number of hotels and private houses have either converted, or have submitted applications for permission to convert into private nursing homes. Sheltered housing for the elderly is presently under construction in Brodick and Lochranza, though in the latter case the name is not very apt as the site has been inundated by floods at least once since building started! Although these facilities provide year-round employment, the conversion of Arran to a 'Granny Farm' would severely damage the summer tourist industry, would put pressure on the local social services (already under considerable strain), and offer little work for the male population of the island. If kept under control, a limited growth of this 'industry' would prove valuable to the island economy, but it should not be allowed to get out of hand.

The oil boom of the 1970s largely passed Arran by, although the presence of some drill rigs moored in Lamlash Bay did fuel rumours of potential discoveries in the Firth of Clyde. Visions of rich oil workers buying or building houses on Arran, and commuting to work by helicopter, filled a few heads at the time, but it turned out that the rigs were merely 'stacked' in Lamlash while waiting for work. Further exploration may yet reveal oil in the area, but it is unlikely that Arran would be a base for any major developments when the much more extensive facilities of towns like Ayr are nearby.

The role of the forestry industry in the future of the island looks to be an expanding one. The yield of timber from the plantings should gradually increase over the next few years, as long as suitable markets can be found. In this respect, the success of industries such as paper-making at Irvine will be of critical importance. If they prosper, then the acres of trees blanketing the moorlands of Arran will become a vital cog in the economy of the island. If, on the other hand, the market for timber should falter, then many will feel that the character of the island has been changed, and not for the better, by futile economics. Those who were outraged by what they saw as the despoliation of beauty in the name of profit will feel their viewpoint justified. That great and doughty campaigner for the island and its ways, the late Miss Bess Macmillan of Brodick, sadly will not be with us to see whether or not the critics were correct.

The danger now is that as the timber is felled, the scars of the extraction process may take a long time to heal if care is not taken to restore the land during the process. If the forests are not to be replanted, then grasses and heathers should be sown on the cleared areas, and every attempt made to minimise any damage to the environment. The saga of Brodick beach and its erosion, no matter where the blame may lie, should be a warning as to what can happen when the balance of nature is disturbed. While the worst fears of the anti-afforestation lobby have not been realised, nevertheless Arran cannot afford to be complacent. Too many beautiful parts of the world are in the process of being ruined by over-exploitation, greed and carelessness already, and Arran should not presume itself immune.

At present the population of Arran is more or less stable in numbers but not in distribution. What is becoming a little alarming to some people is the increasing concentration of shops, banks and other economic facilities in Brodick. Two small shopping developments have opened up in the village, near the pier, with a view to attracting small craft shops to move there. To date this project has met with mixed success, but the thinking behind it is interesting, and has raised a few objections from elsewhere on the island from people worried about maintaining the smaller communities as viable concerns. If too many of the economic developments become centred in Brodick, there is a danger that the rest of the island will atrophy. This may well suit some of the people who have moved to Arran looking for their retirement idyll, but it will do little for the long-term economic and social health of the island.

Again, Arran will wither and die if development and change are stifled. The recent expansion of the Arran Provisions factory, for example, is a great boost for the island, and will, it is hoped, continue to provide employment opportunities for local people for many years to come. But less welcome is the controversy surrounding developments which exploit local resources to the possible detriment of the environment, such as gravel extraction from the beaches, the sand pit near the Home Farm by Brodick, and the expansion of the fish farm at Lamlash. In such situations Arran faces the same dilemma as many other parts of the Scottish Highlands and Islands today: whether to take advantage of current trends and fashions and exploit local resources, possibly to the long-term detriment of the environment, or to sacrifice potential job opportunities in exchange for the maintenance of a period piece. It is not an easy choice, and it is little wonder that the local attitudes and opinions as to the merits of tourism are somewhat mixed.

Arran today is in just as much of a boundary position between the Highland and Lowland ways of life as ever it was. The eastern villages such as Brodick, Lamlash and Whiting Bay are part of the Firth of Clyde resort chain, while the villages of the west still retain that slight air of the glorious balmy days of the 1930s when summers were hot and the pressures of modern living were no more than the foreshadowings of science fiction. The distinctive sense of timelessness that is one of the essentials of the Arran experience is still alive and living between Catacol and Kildonan. Let us hope it will never be extinguished by the hustle of the mainland, despite the gradual spread of granny-farms, coach tours and industry along the eastern seaboard of the island.

It may be that some time in the future, when the helicopter becomes as common as the family car is in the 1980s, Arran will become a commuter paradise for busy Glaswegians. Until that day, the sea helps to shield the island and its inhabitants from the rigours and, it must be said, from many of the benefits of mainland life. Possible changes to the tourist industry cannot be ruled out, especially if the whispered threat of local landowners that they intend to levy a charge for geologists to visit sites on their land is implemented. Should such a decision cause the student parties that currently herald the beginning of the 'season' to look elsewhere for their field trips, the viability of a number of the hotels on the island might be called into question. Whatever happens, Arran is like anywhere else in that it cannot totally insulate itself from the tides of change which sweep the land from time to time. So much depends on factors outside the island over which the locals can exercise no control.

However, should each succeeding generation of children, whether local or visitor, discover the joys of wandering the Arran lanes between the hedgerows or drystone dykes looking for brambles in the perfect evening light at the end of a summer's day, or stand breathless in the wind on the summit of Goatfell watching the antics of ravens and eagles in the sky above, or dash through the breakers on a sunny beach, or even sit entranced over a jigsaw puzzle while the rain hammers at the window, the magic of Arran will remain.

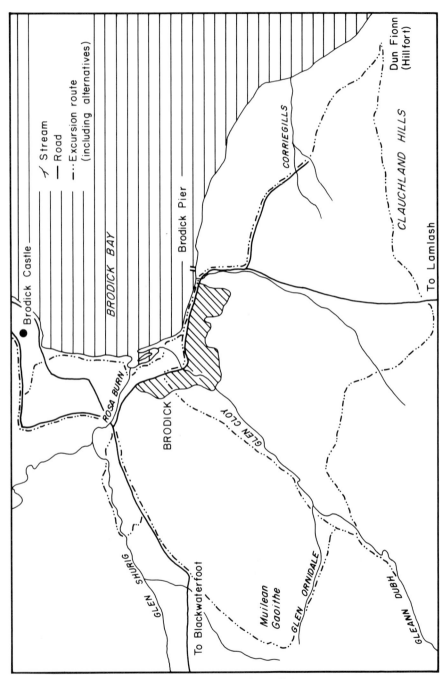

Excursion 1. The round Brodick tour.

The Round Brodick Tour

This excursion is best suited to walkers, though some parts of the route can be followed in a car. The walking, although a little rough in parts, follows paths, tracks and roads for most of the distance, but there is a section of bout 2 km which is rather more steep and rugged. This part, though, can be missed out to leave a rather gentler walk. The complete route covers about 15 km, but can be broken up into a series of shorter sections.

The route starts and ends at Brodick pier (NS 022360), making this a convenient route for the visitor who comes across on the ferry and wants to do no more than explore a little of the Brodick area. From the pier, turn left onto the main road to Lamlash and follow it up the hill past the garden centre on the right. After a short distance a minor road signposed to Strathwhillan branches off to the left, but this is a dead-end and you should continue up the main road until another road branches off to the left. This road is signposted to Corriegills, and several signs at the junction indicate the presence of woodcarvers, basketmakers and other craft workshops along this road. Turn left and walk or drive up the hill towards Corriegills, a small hamlet (NS 032348) tucked away beneath the forested slopes of the Clauchland Hills. It is worthwhile taking time while walking or driving up this hill to turn and look northwards, once you have gained some altitude, where in good weather there is a spectacular view of Brodick Bay and the north Arran mountains, dominated by Goatfell and the ridge of the Sleeping Warrior.

Corriegills itself is notable for little except a sense of rural tranquillity and good views of the Clauchland Hills. Follow the road through the hamlet, ignoring a side-road on the left, until the road dips to cross a bridge (NS 034346). As the road beyond is largely unsurfaced and leads only to a few houses, cars should be left at this point unless it is intended to visit the woodcarvers' premises, about 0.5 km beyond the bridge. Follow the track as it winds between luxuriant hedgerows and beneath the branches of overhanging trees for about 1 km. Almost immediately before reaching the last cottage on the track, a sign pointing to Dun Fionn and Lamlash directs the walker up a poorly defined path around the back of the cottage. After pushing through gorse, crossing a small stream and passing over a stile, the route becomes much clearer, a path leading diagonally up the slopes of the Clauchland Hills. Just before the path reaches the crest of the hills a track branches off it to the left (east) and leads, after a short but steep climb, to the ancient hill fort called Dun Fionn. Of the fort, which is possibly Iron Age in origin, little can be seen except a flattened floor and low ridges in the turf, marking what are probably the outer walls. As the fort is perched on the top of a cliff, care should be taken not to go too close to the eastern end, especially if wearing footwear with fairly smooth soles. Even from the safe centre of the fort the views are spectacular. To the north Goatfell and the other peaks fill the view, while the great sweep of the Firth of Clyde and the Ayrshire coast is spread out to the east. To the south, Lamlash Bay and Holy Isle form a most attractive picture, and it is only to the west that the view is blocked by rising ground.

The route now turns west along the crest of the Clauchland Hills. From Dun Fionn a path leads more or less along the crest of the ridge, with spectacular views both to north and south The path is quite well marked, but the hills have been planted with trees which can sometimes obscure the twists and turns of the route, especially during the descent towards the main road at the western end of the ridge. Just beside the point where the path reaches the main road there is a stone circle (NS 019335) of granite blocks. These are quite small, and the circle may be difficult to see if the heather has been growing vigorously.

Those to whom the route thus far has given all the exercise they want can turn onto the main road and, turning right, follow the highway back to Brodick pier. Those who still have the energy to go further should cross the main road at its very summit between Lamlash and Brodick, and enter the Forest Walk that is signposted there. Picnic tables are discreetly hidden in the trees a short distance along the Walk from the main road. The route of the Forest Walk should be followed for the next two to three km as it winds round the flank of a

Felling operations in the forests blanketing the hills between Brodick and Lamlash are watched over by the 'Sleeping Warrior' — the mountain ridge named for its appearance when viewed from the Ayrshire coast.

hill, and descends towards Glen Cloy. Although excellent views of the Goatfell massif can still be glimpsed through the trees, the main interest here is the gradual opening up of the view of Glen Cloy and the two steep valleys at its head, Glen Dubh and Glen Ormidale.

The Forest Walk should be followed down into Glen Cloy and across the Cloy Burn to where it joins a rather muddy footpath along the glen. Here a short detour to the left, upvalley, will reveal some scenes of interest to those who are fascinated by both the history of Arran and the Ice Age in Arran. The path leads over a series of mounds and ridges on the floor of the glen until suddenly it stops on the crest of the highest of these ridges. Beyond this point the valley floor suddenly becomes very flat, marking the area where there was a lake during the Ice Age. This lake, which has now completely infilled with silt, had been dammed up by the ridges which themselves were formed by the action of glacier ice advancing down from the moorlands at the head of the glen. The scene must have been very spectacular then, with a river of ice possibly pouring down the steep wall at the head of Glen Dubh, pushing into the sands and gravels on the bed of the valley and contorting and reworking them to leave the mounds and ridges visible nowadays.

One of the mounds on the floor of Glen Dubh had an ancient fort on its crest (NR 992339). This site, obscured nowadays by trees, was largely cleared sometime in the late eighteenth or nineteenth century, possibly to provide material for drystone dykes, but it is thought that it may have been the fort to which the followers of Robert the Bruce are supposed to have retreated following their attack on the garrison of Brodick Castle.

Retracing the path downvalley to the junction with the Forest Walk, the route now enters its roughest phase. Those who might want to retain the air in their lungs a little longer can follow the footpath down Glen Cloy to join a track returning to Brodick village. The remainder should turn west, into Glen Ormidale, and follow the stream that drains through the glen up its rather steep course to the point at which the valley opens out onto a broad plateau with some peat hags. Turn north and follow the ridge to the summit of Muilean Caoithe (NR 983351), where spectacular views can be enjoyed over Glen Cloy, the Firth of Clyde and the northern granite mountains.

The route now lies to the north, towards the narrow ribbon of the String Road which links Brodick with the area around Blackwaterfoot. The descent from Muilean Caiothe should be taken with some care as it is quite steep for the first part, but thereafter it is simply a case of striking out across the moor to join the String Road at a convenient point. The road can then be followed down the flanks of Glen Shurig and past the old Brodick burial ground to the junction with the main road round the island just outside Brodick (NS 005368). A slightly quieter and more scenic alternative is to follow the String downwards only as far as the track down to West Glensherraig and the other farms sprinkled along the floor of Glen Shurig. Paths and rough tracks provide a pleasant walk along the Glen and link ultimately to the metalled road from Glen Rosa to Brodick. Turn right on this road, and follow it along to its junction with the String Road, where the detour rejoins the main route.

Those whose feet are not too sore, and who are inclined to explore a little farther, should turn left at the foot of the String Road where it joins the main road around the island and cross the Rosa Burn by a picturesque humpbacked bridge. Immediately beyond the bridge turn left through a gateway, and a smooth road can then be followed through the fields and woodlands that form part of the policies of Brodick Castle. The road affords lovely views into the entrance to Glen Rosa and up Glen Shurig, but as it approaches the castle it enters more wooded countryside, laid out by the National Trust as a series of trails and recreational areas.

Brodick Castle and its gardens are a most worthwhile visit in their own right, the castle with its elegant rooms and works of art, and the gardens containing a range of exotic and colourful plants that is the equal of any of the other famous gardens of the west coast of Scotland. The excursion route, however, passes around the back of the castle and descends through the paddocks and trees to the coast on the north side of Brodick Bay. Turn right, and head back along the coast, past the tiny harbour which used to serve the castle, to the site of the sawmill at Cladach. Here a collection of craft shops has grown up using the old buildings marking the site of the original village of Brodick before it was re-established on the south side of the bay in the mid-nineteenth century.

The return to Brodick can then be made either by following the main road or, more picturesquely, by walking along the beach beside Brodick golf course. The mouth of the Rosa Burn is crossed by a footbridge, as is the Cloy Burn just behind Brodick Beach. At the mouth of the Rosa, the keen birdwatcher can spot, depending on the time of year, gulls, swans, geese, terns, swallows and martins as well as herons and the occasional bird of prey. If the walker is not tempted to stop and bathe aching feet in the sea, the main road is regained more or less in the centre of Brodick, just beside the putting green. Then it is only a short walk along the front past the hotels and shops to return to the starting point of the excursion at Brodick pier.

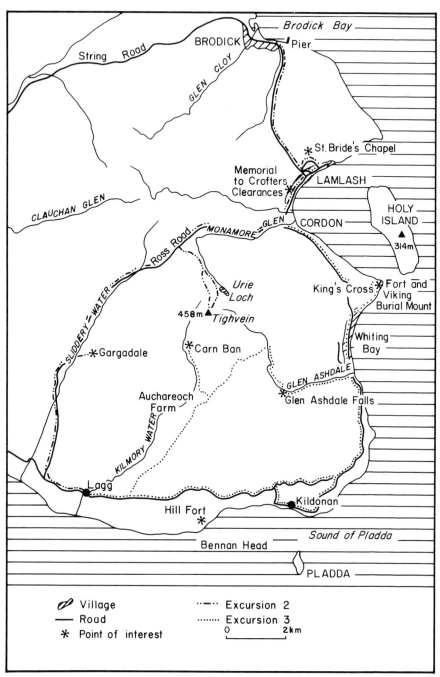

Excursions 2 and 3. The south of the island.

EXCURSION 2

Lamlash to Lagg via the Ross Road

This excursion is well suited to car-borne explorers of the island, though walkers will find the route a rewarding experience if a little sore on the feet. For the walker, this route is in quite remote countryside even if it does lie along a road, and it would be as well to take a supply of food on the trip as there will be few opportunities to buy any, once Lamlash is left behind. Cyclists also may enjoy this excursion, though all but the strongest thighs will wilt a little following the Ross Road.

The route starts at the clubhouse of Lamlash Golf Course, situated to the east of the road from Brodick just as it enters Lamlash (NS 026320). Follow the main road down the hill for about 100 m to where a small road joins it at a sharp angle from the east (NS 029318). Take this very sharp turn to the left and follow the road down into a hollow and up again, crossing the golf course, until a sign appears for the burial ground and the ruins of the Chapel of St Bride, a pre-Reformation structure. The graveyard, situated on a pleasant site looking out over Lamlash Bay to Holy Isle, contains a number of sculptured stones and other monuments of interest which may detain the traveller for a while.

The route should then be retraced to join the main road, which is followed down the hill and into Lamlash. Cyclists should beware of the sharp bend at the foot of the hill where the main road turns right (west) along the beach. About 100 m west of the turn in the road, on the left there is a bowling green behind which is a sandstone clock tower which is all that is left of the so-called 'new' pier at Lamlash. This is where the ferries used to call, until it was finally closed in 1954. Another 100 m along the road will take you to the Old Pier Cafe, beside which a lane leads to the old stone-built pier which is still sometimes used by fishing and small cargo boats. Beside the Old Pier are the concrete ramps on which many of the boats belonging to the Arran Yacht Club, based in Lamlash, are drawn up. In the summer, in particular, the waters around the Old Pier are dotted with moored yachts and other pleasure

157

boats, taking advantage of the shelter provided by Holy Isle.

As you walk from the main road along the alley towards the Old Pier, you will see notices advertising fishing tackle, boat hire and bait. Lamlash is a noted centre of sea angling and has hosted an annual festival for the brotherhood of the rod for a number of years. On a slightly different scale, a careful look towards the south-east side of the bay may reveal the low outline of a fish farm, the subject of considerable dispute among the local population.

At one time a ferry used to operate from the Old Pier to Holy Isle, where a short walk would take the visitor to St Molio's Cave (NS 060295). Wild goats live on the island, and among its other attractions are two lighthouses and some splendid views of Arran. Sadly, the present owners of the island have discouraged visitors, and the ferry no longer runs.

Continuing towards the centre of Lamlash, a stone monument is seen in a small grassy area in front of the attractive row of former estate cottages forming Hamilton Terrace (NS 026312). A plaque on the monument indicates that it commemorates the departure in 1829 from the island of the former inhabitants of North Glen Sannox, cleared from their houses to make way for sheep, and setting out to try and construct a new life for themselves in Canada.

Lamlash is the main administrative centre for the island, and as you proceed southwards along the main road, you pass in rapid succession the main health centre on the island, the police station and, on the right-hand side, Arran High School. Crossing the narrow Arranton Bridge just beyond the school (NS 024305), a narrow road branches off to the left, leading to the little clachan of Cordon, still a separate settlement but almost swallowed up as Lamlash expands southwards. The route stays on the main road, passing the modern private estate houses on the outskirts of Lamlash, to the junction with the Ross Road (NS 019302) beside the new Arran Provisions factory. Visitors are welcome here, and there is a shop where samples of the produce can be bought.

Branching right (west) onto the Ross Road, the route rapidly narrows and starts to climb quite sharply, at first past fields, then through birch woodland and onto the steep slopes of the Monamore Glen. The floor of the glen, far below, can be

The view eastwards down the Monamore Glen towards Holy Isle from the top of the Ross Road has changed greatly over the last decade as the lower slopes of the hills have become swathed in coniferous forest, in places growing to such an extent as to restrict the view.

glimpsed through gaps in the plantations of trees which cover the lower slopes of the glen. At the top of the road, the scenery changes to an open moorland, with an extensive view back down the Monamore Glen to Holy Isle and beyond, to the Ayrshire coast. From here the keen walker can easily walk across the moors and the peat hags to visit some of the wilder and less visited parts of the south end of the island. One particular site of interest is the Urie Loch (NS 002280), a small body of water perched on the high plateau above the Ross Road, a visit to which could be combined with the ascent of Tighvein (NR 998274), the highest point on the island south of the Ross Road.

The route then follows the Ross Road south-westwards, descending via a number of very sharp bends which might trap the unwary driver. Much of this area is now being afforested, but the sense of loneliness is not relieved until the route approaches the one habitation in the upper glen, Glenscorrodale Farm (NR 963280), where afternoon tea can usually be obtained in the summer months. From here the

The Lagg Inn is one of the oldest hotels on Arran, dating from the early nineteenth century, in the latter part of which it was linked to the east-coast steamer ports by one of the earliest scheduled coach services on the island.

route follows the glen, which gradually becomes more open and less enclosed, and the moorland starts to give way to pasture.

From a number of vantage points on the road, by looking across the glen to the eastern slopes, the ruins of a number of buildings can be seen. This is the abandoned village of Gargadale (NR 957262), emptied of its population in the Clearances. It can be a rather emotional experience to cross the valley and climb to Gargadale, wandering round the ruins in this lonely spot as the birds cry overhead, just as they must have done when the place was a bustling settlement.

The route continues to follow the Ross Road southwards, winding downhill to cross Sliddery Water at a picturesque little site beside the ruins of an old mill (NR 946245). South from here the road crosses undulating open ground with large, regularly-shaped fields, relics of the enclosures of the early nineteenth century. Traces of the old rigs which predated the enclosures are still preserved on some of the steeper slopes leading down to Sliddery Water, just to the west of the road (e.g. at NR 945241), where they are best seen towards evening when the setting sun throws shadows which reveal them quite clearly.

The view in this area is very extensive, reaching out across the waters of the Firth of Clyde to Kintyre and beyond to the coast of Northern Ireland (at least in fine weather). The atmosphere of the whole region is now much less dramatic, and instead is a rather peaceful, pastoral scene, typical of much of south-west Arran.

The route soon reaches the other end of the Ross Road, where it joins the main road round the island beside a solitary church (NR 942221). Turn left (eastwards) and follow the main road across rolling pasture to Lagg, the destination for this excursion. Lagg itself is a delightful spot, approached by a very steep and twisting descent into the valley of the Kilmory Water (NR 955216). Here, trees (including palm trees) and flowers grow abundantly in the shelter and mild atmosphere of the valley, providing an almost bewildering contrast with the open pastures only a short distance away. The Lagg Hotel, situated in this valley with lawns running down to the river, provides welcome rest and refreshment after the rigours of the excursion. There can be few things on Arran more enjoyable than to sit on a wall beside the river at Lagg in the late afternoon sun, recuperating before the return journey to Lamlash or wherever.

The return to the starting point of the excursion in Lamlash can be made by continuing along the main road round the island, the details of which are listed as Excursion 3.

Lamlash to Lagg via Whiting Bay

There are really two routes within this excursion. One of them follows the road, and is therefore suitable for all wheeled traffic as well as walkers. The other branches off the main route, and thereafter follows a series of forest tracks, suitable only for cross-country vehicles for much of their length, before rejoining the main route just before it reaches Lagg.

The excursion begins at the junction of the Ross Road and the main road around the island, beside the Arran Provisions factory (NS 019302), the route following the main road over the bridge and winding up through the woodlands with ever-expanding views over Lamlash Bay and Holy Isle. About halfway up this ascent, a signpost pointing to the left (north) indicates the presence of the 'Cuddy Dook', a path leading down the steep slope to the hamlet of Cordon. The origin of the name 'Cuddy Dook' is uncertain, but the two favourite theories are either that it relates to the fact that when on horseback (a horse is a 'cuddy' in much of the West of Scotland) the rider would have to duck ('dook') to pass beneath the branches of the trees which overhang the path, or that it indicates the route by which the 'cuddies' were taken to be 'dooked' in the sea to wash them.

Onwards to the south the route levels out, with vistas northwards across Lamlash Bay, now revealing the Goatfell massif behind the village, and southwards the huge expanse of the Firth of Clyde with the Ayrshire hills beyond. After about 1 km a branch road on the left (east) signposted to King's Cross and the 'Viking Fort' promises an interesting diversion from the main route. Follow the road through all its contortions across pleasant farm country, and then continue on footpaths and small tracks along the coast towards Kingscross Point (NS 056283). At Kingscross Point a path leads up past the rusting remnants of a World War Two gun emplacement into the remains of an Iron Age broch, now visible as a more or less circular wall about 10 m in diameter. A short distance to the south-west, the path cuts through whins and brambles which

Glen Ashdale Falls, the highest on the island, can now be viewed from a recently constructed observation platform, part of a network of viewpoints and paths in the area.

effectively conceal the rocks of a Viking grave mound, in which several interesting artifacts, including a bronze coin, were found when it was excavated at the beginning of this century. The reference on the signpost at the main road is actually a mistake, based on a false linking of the Viking and the Iron Age remains at the one site.

You return to the main road, either by retracing your steps or, if no vehicle is involved, by walking south-east along a shore path that leads back to the main road at the north end of the village of Whiting Bay. Whichever the route, the next point of interest on the excursion is Whiting Bay village itself. The route follows the main road along the coast, passing through this attractive village with its safe beaches, palm trees and wooded hilly backdrop. On the way through the village, note the number of craft shops and signs pointing to workshops, often situated up steep winding tracks above the village. The centre of the village (NS 045262) is where the pier used to be until the cost of upkeep led to its closure in 1957 and subsequent demolition.

Follow the road southwards through the village until the bridge over the Glenashdale Burn (NS 046253) is reached, beside a youth hostel. A track leads off up the south side of the glen, immediately over the bridge, and is signposted to Glenashdale Falls. These Falls, the highest in Arran, with a triple cascade descending some 40 m into a wooded defile, are well worth a visit, especially now that the paths have been improved, and new viewing platforms constructed so that the Falls can be better appreciated. The walk is not difficult, but may be a little muddy in wet weather.

While motorists will retrace their steps to the main road in order to continue the excursion, walkers or possessors of mountain bikes have an alternative they can now select. If, instead of returning to the main road, you continue to follow the paths up Glenashdale, by crossing a bridge over the river above the falls, your track will lead on to join a forest track. Turn left at the junction, and follow this track through the forestry plantations past little waterfalls and some grassy meadows until eventually you will come to the farm called Auchareoch (NR 994245). A short distance north of this farm, another forest track, signposted to Carn Ban, branches

The forces of nature are still active on Arran. Here reinforcements are being placed to protect the coast road at Kildonan from erosion by the sea.

westwards off your route. Those with an interest in archaeology should follow this track, and the signposted footpath that branches northwards soon after the junction will lead them after a rather damp plod past the plantations to the mound of stones called Carn Ban, one of the finest Neolithic burial cairns in Arran.

From Auchareoch, another track leads south-west, through the trees and up onto the open moorland of southern Arran, a rather monotonous landscape relieved by huge views to the south encompassing Kintyre, the Rhinns of Galloway, Ailsa Craig and (if lucky) the Antrim coast. Follow this track to rejoin the main road some 2 km east of Lagg.

Having regained the main road in Whiting Bay, those who are following the coastal variant of the excursion should travel south, past Cooper Angus caravan park and along the coast road towards the clachan of Largybeg (NS 050234), rising steadily as you progress. Just to the south of Largybeg there is a substantial layby where you can stop and admire the views out over the Firth of Clyde to Ayrshire, while below a couple of whitewashed cottages sit by the shore. If the road up here looks in a poor state of maintenance it is because the route is crossing a landslip which is still occasionally active and causes the road surface to break up from time to time.

Just south of this viewpoint, the road turns sharply to the west, and the scenery changes completely. Instead of the steep slopes dropping to the waters of the Firth of Clyde, now the route runs across the high plateaux of the south of the island, and the main focal points for the view centre on Kintyre and on the massive presence of Ailsa Craig sitting in the middle of the Firth. The plateaux are cut by streams flowing in small gorges, and the roads have to make many sharp turns to cross them. This is not a route for the careless driver to undertake lightly!

Passing Dippin Lodge (NS 050223), a hunting lodge built by the Hamiltons in the nineteenth century, partly hidden among the trees to the left of the route, you soon come to a road junction. Take the minor route to the south, signposted to Kildonan, and follow it through a small wooded valley to emerge on a hillslope overlooking the south coast of Arran and, about a kilometre offshore, the strange flat shape of the island of Pladda, with its lighthouse (NS 028190).

Follow the road down towards the coast, and you enter the village of Kildonan (NS 030207), rather more of a scatter of houses and a couple of hotels than a compact settlement. The ruins of the fourteenth century castle (NS 037209) are dangerous and should not be approached too closely, but the situation is superb — perched on a low clifftop overlooking one of the better sandy beaches on the island. Westwards, other sandy beaches fringe the coast, separated from each other by the low natural rock walls or dykes, objects of considerable interest to geologists. Kildonan is a charming spot for a picnic and a swim, with the dramatic cliff scenery of Bennan Head a short distance to the west as a backdrop.

The route turns away from the coast, climbing steeply beside a gorge to rejoin the main road. Turn left (west) and continue towards Bennan Head, on the flanks of which the marks of old ploughrigs can be seen. Looking back down to the east there is a stunning view across Kildonan and Pladda to the Ayrshire coast some 25 km across the Firth of Clyde. The route west follows the road across undramatic pasture lands amidst which are built some of the highest houses in Arran. Soon the junction with the walkers' track is reached (NR 969214), after which the road rapidly drops towards the village of Kilmory, passing on the left (south) the Torrylinn Creamery (NR 962215) where the Arran cheese is produced. This cheese is a tasty souvenir of a visit to the island, but can sometimes be difficult to obtain locally, as much of the production is sold abroad.

For the traveller, by this time getting rather weary, there is only one major problem to negotiate before the welcoming sight of the Lagg Hotel appears in its sheltered valley, and that is the very steep and twisting road down into the valley. This is every bit as 'exhilarating' as the road on the west side of Lagg, and should be negotiated with care. Once Lagg is reached, and such refreshments as are felt necessary are consumed, then the return to Lamlash may be made either by retracing the route or by travelling a short distance farther west and then returning via the Ross Road (Excursion 2).

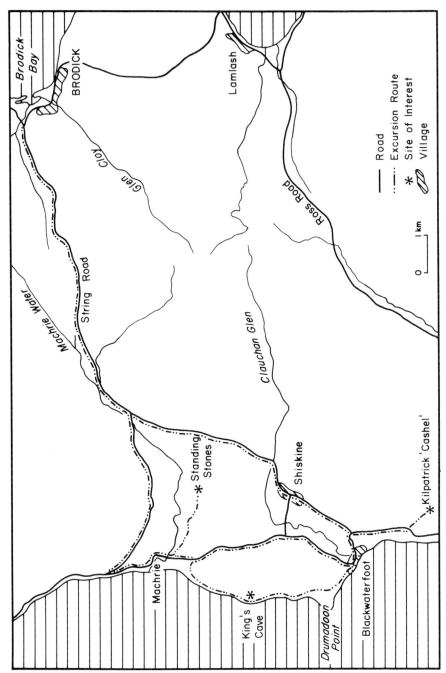

Excursion 4. Machrie and Blackwaterfoot.

EXCURSION 4

Brodick and the Shiskine Valley

For the motorist, this excursion and its attendant diversions on foot to explore aspects of this region should not prove too exhausting, but for the walker, the idea of taking a bus over the String Road at least as far as the Machrie Road junction (NR 932340) may help to keep this day pleasant and not excessively strenuous.

Starting from Brodick pier, travel westwards through the village of Brodick, keeping to the main road. Note the prehistoric standing stone on the north side of the road opposite the primary school (NS 010367). Less than 100 m farther along the main road is the Arran Heritage Museum, well worth a visit to see exhibitions of all sorts of aspects of past life on the island. Also in this area it is worth keeping an eye open for red squirrels which live in the surrounding woods.

The route forks left (west) off the main road just outside the village of Brodick (NS 005368), and starts to follow the String Road uphill past the old Brodick graveyard towards the moors. The String Road (named, according to one story, after the Norse for a cord, though this sheds little light on the origin of the name) rises rapidly towards the head of Glen Shurig, the slope presenting a real challenge to a heavily laden car, never mind a cyclist. At the summit of the road (NR 977359) a panoramic view can be enjoyed. To the east, the waters of the Firth of Clyde are spread out below rather like an animated map on which ships plough back and forth, while to the north the dramatic peaks of the Arran hills rise sharply from a boggy plateau. To the south, a steep slope rises and blocks the view, but to the west the length of Gleann ant-Suidhe beckons the observer towards the Kilbrannan Sound with views of distant Kintyre.

Paralleling the road down Gleann ant-Suidhe, traces of the old drove road used in the past for driving cattle over to market at Brodick or to the ferry can be seen on the north side of the glen. Stay with the String Road, and you will emerge into rather wider and more fertile valleys farmed from stone-built farmhouses sheltering beneath the slopes or among the trees which become more common now that lower ground has been reached. The north side of the valley is isolated from the road by a high wire fence, erected to try and contain the red deer and stop them from damaging trees and crops in the more fertile southern half of the island. This fence extends right across the island, but stiles or gates through it are provided on most of the more popular walking routes.

The route comes to a fork where the String Road meets a minor road signposted to Machrie (NR 932340). Here, those who have taken the bus should disembark. The first thing that catches the eye here, apart from the glowering scree slopes just to the south-east, is the elaborately carved sandstone pillarbox. This ornate object looks as though it must have some exotic history but is in fact a folly, less than a hundred years old. Leaving behind human follies, the route follows the minor road across the bridge over Machrie Water, one of the better stretches of private fishing on Arran, and passes through birch woodland to emerge in an area of pasture. The deer fence is crossed via a noisy cattle grid, and the route then winds across an area of moorland, much of which is in the process of afforestation. Extensive views southwards show that the route is skirting the northern margins of the Shiskine Valley, the largest area of fertile lowland on the island. Follow the route onwards as it descends gently to the coast of the Kilbrannan Sound at Machrie, where you should turn left (southwards) at the junction with the main road.

Follow the main road southwards along the coast past Machrie Golf Club (an excellent place for afternoon tea in summer) and inland between the hedgerows and the whins for about 2 km to where a sign points at a farm track (NR 894330) leading to Machrie Moor and the standing stones. Cars can be parked in a small area opposite the beginning of the track, but care should be taken not to leave vehicles blocking farm gates or tracks. In any conditions except near drought this is a very muddy path, and Wellingtons or equivalent boots are strongly recommended. The walk out onto the moor is about 2 km, the first part of which lies across farmland, but later climbs slightly onto low moorland before dropping down to the main group of stone circles. Small boards have been erected by each of the

The great bulk of Beinn Nuis looms over the String Road as it crosses the centre of the island.

main groups of standing stones and other monuments which give the details of the various structures, but the overall effect, especially when standing below a 5 m-high standing stone on a grey misty day, is a sense of timelessness, almost as though the builders of these monuments might at any moment emerge from the mists and resume their rituals of worship.

Return to the road, and follow it south for about 500 m. Here (NR 895325) a signpost to the right (west) indicates a track to the King's Cave. This is not a route for vehicles, and car drivers would do better to visit the caves from Blackwaterfoot, where they can park their car more easily before walking to the caves. For walkers, though, it can be made into a pleasant through route, if the track is followed to the beach at Machrie, and then some rather muddy paths followed southwards to the caves (NR 884310). There is doubt whether or not the caves around here were ever used by Robert the Bruce, as the legend claims, but there are some interesting carvings of possible early Christian and Pictish origin in the King's Cave itself. From there the walker should follow a well-marked path southwards along the coast, then bypass the cliff on the inland side to avoid any difficulties. The opportunity can be taken while here to climb up to look at the extensive ramparts of the massive hill fort of Drumadoon

171

Many of the island villages hold festivals during the summer months, at which displays of local talents and skills are mixed with those of visitors and invited guests. Here dinghies in 'fancy dress' take part in a competition at the Lochranza Gala Day.

(NR 884292) before rejoining the path and descending to the coast at Blackwaterfoot golf course and the magnificent sandy sweep of the adjacent beach.

Meanwhile, vehicle drivers will have driven southwards along the road through moorlands and pasture lands, the latter scattered with daffodils and other blooms in spring, while in May and June the hawthorn blossoms on the hedges bordering the roads bring another touch of colour to a verdant scene. As you approach the village of Blackwaterfoot, newly built private houses become more common, especially where the sites offer vantage points looking out over Kilbrannan Sound to Kintyre, or north-east over the green lowlands of the Shiskine Valley to the distant granite peaks in the north of the island. At the bottom of the steep descent to the coast turn right onto the minor road (NR 893283) and follow it for about 500 m towards the private car park for the golf course. Vehicles can be parked on the approach to the golf course. From there, signposted footpaths direct the energetic along the coast to King's Cave,

A parade of sports cars attracts the attention of villagers in Pirnmill. Notice that even on the windswept west coast of Arran, trees can grow well if shelter is available.

while on a warm summer day the attractions of the safe sandy beach become apparent.

The walkers' and the drivers' routes now coincide, and should be followed back to the main road, and then through the village of Blackwaterfoot, with its attractive little harbour. Hotels and shops here will allow the traveller to replenish stocks of food, energy, film or other necessities for the enjoyment of an excursion. The route then lies eastward until the junction (NR 902284) with the foot of the String Road, here signposted to Brodick.

Before turning onto the String Road for the return journey, a detour may be made southwards along the main road to Kilpatrick (NR 903268), where a signpost will direct the walker towards 'Kilpatrick Dun', a short distance up a side track. Here are the remains of an enclosed area and a circular building, possibly a tower. The *Book of Arran* thought it might be an early monastic site, hence its marking as a Cashel on the Ordnance Survey map, but it may equally well be an earlier defensive site. Whatever its origin, it commands a splendid outlook to

Kintyre, Drumadoon and the Shiskine Valley and the northern hills. Having explored the site, it is then time to return to the excursion route proper.

As you turn northwards onto the String Road, the route now runs across some of the most fertile ground on Arran, tucked in beneath the slopes of the southern moorlands, slopes which are nowadays extensively afforested. There is an almost continuous ribbon of houses along the first 2 km of the String Road here, including the village of Shiskine, the only substantial inland village in Arran. On the way to Shiskine the route passes by St Molio's Church (NR 909295), built in 1889, but of interest for the monumental effigy of an abbot built into the west Hall. Transported from the site of an earlier church at Clachan, this may be thirteenth century and is among the oldest effigies known in the West Highlands.

Continue north through the village, noting on the way the old inn, now turned into a field studies centre (a sign of the changed priorities of modern times), negotiate a couple of sharp bends and the steep bridge over the Clauchan Water (NR 920304). A short distance along a track on the north side of the stream are the ruins of the Clachan church, built about 1805 to replace an older structure on the same site, and its associated graveyard. This was the site from which the effigy in St. Molio's Church was taken.

From here, the route lies north, following the String Road along the eastern side of the valley, through increasingly rough pasture lands and back to the junction with the Machrie Road at the carved postbox. The String Road should then be followed back over the hills to Brodick.

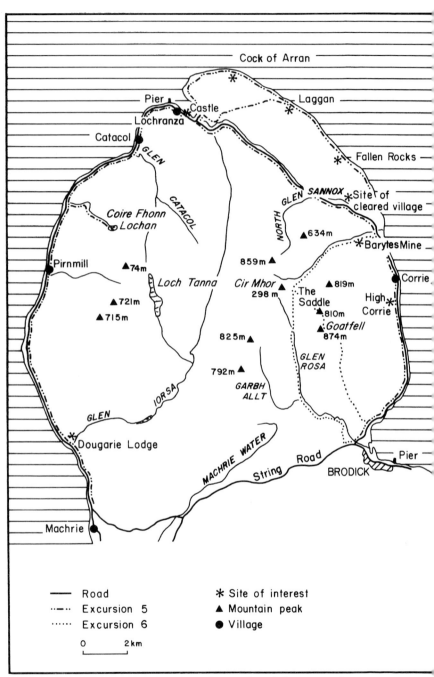

Excursions 5 and 6. The north and the mountains.

The North End of Arran

This excursion is primarily suited to the vehicle-based tourist in its length and in that it uses the main road around the island to a large extent. The walker would do better to think of breaking this down into a series of shorter excursions and to add a little variety to the monotonous diet of tarmac routeway, a couple of alternative routes suitable only for the pedestrian or (possibly) the owner of a mountain bicycle, are presented en route.

From Brodick the route follows the main road northwards out of the village, following signs for Corrie and Lochranza and taking the right-hand road at the junction with the String Road (NS 005378). Follow the road past the little settlement of Cladach and along the coast road beyond the old quay below Brodick Castle. The route follows the coast northwards for the next five to six km, running along the surface of a raised beach marking the sea-level about 5,500 years ago. Note the old cliffline at the inland margin of the beach. The low rocky coast here is an ideal area in which to spot wildlife, with ducks (particularly eider and shelduck) common at some times of the year, as well as herons, shags, cormorants and seals.

As the route is followed northwards, gradually the old cliffs fall back from the road, opening up a view of the Goatfell range of hills rising steeply above the road. Note the large granite boulder perched atop the old cliffline just south of Corrie (NS 024421). This is Clach Mhor (the big stone), said to weigh some 620 tons, and thought to have been dropped in place by glaciers during the last Ice Age.

On crossing the bridge over the Corrie Burn, foaming down from the slopes of Goatfell, a jeep track branches off the main road (NS 025423). A short walk up this track will take you to the charming clachan known as High Corrie (NS 022424), a collection of whitewashed croft houses scattered across a meadow below the boulder-clad slopes of the mountains. This settlement, a haunt of artists and writers for many years, commands spectacular views over the Firth of Clyde and along the coast of Arran.

The next settlement is Corrie itself, possibly the most attractive village on Arran, with clear relics of its past glories as an exporter of building stone. Entering the village, a series of local authority houses are passed and behind them can be seen a great hole in the old cliffline. This marks the spot where the sandstone was quarried, and then taken by tramway to the 'new' harbour (NS 026428), still with a last load of sandstone blocks waiting to be taken away. The most picturesque part of the village lies north of the 'new' harbour. Here crouches a row of old cottages with a maze of greenery cloaking the steep slopes behind. In the midst of this part of the village is the 'old' harbour (NS 024437), a delightful little anchorage which was used in part to aid the export of limestone quarried from the caves in the hillslope behind. These caves are still visible, but they are dangerous, and should not be entered.

Leaving Corrie, the route follows the main road north to Sannox, passing on the way the great granite boulder called the Cat Stone (NS 019447), legendary site of a skirmish between some islanders and a group of Cromwellian soldiers, the latter coming off the worse in the encounter. Sannox itself is a pleasant small group of houses, overlooking a sandy bay and commanding splendid views of the north Arran mountains which here seem to tower over the road. A path signposted to Glen Sannox will lead the walker to the site of the old barytes processing plant (NS 009452), and little piles of spoil and some fenced-off mineshafts can still be seen marking the extent of the former workings.

Crossing the bridge over the Sannox Burn, it is worth taking another brief detour from the road, this time to visit Sannox Church (NS 017456), which is reached by going through a signposted gateway on the right (east) side of the road and walking up a short pathway. It is of interest from a historical viewpoint as well as being architecturally distinctive, for it was built in 1822 as an independent congregationalist church by the local people following the Haldane brothers' mission to the district in 1800.

The route follows the main road north from Sannox over the hill into North Glen Sannox. Here, walkers may part company with their motorised brethren. The main route follows the road to Lochranza over the pass called the Boguillie, passing through glens with excellent views of the granite peaks, in particular of the dramatic gash of the Witches Step (NR 977444) cleaving a ridge above North Glen Sannox to a depth of 100 m, and it has numerous other features of interest including the site of the cleared village of North Glen Sannox, now little more than piles of stones on the floor on the glen (NS 002467), a rather sad and lonely place especially in the quiet stillness of a summer evening. The descent from the top of the Boguillie is often enlivened by glimpses of deer in the valley, and on rare occasions by the majestic patrolling flight of a golden eagle. Take the road down the hill into Lochranza, the scattered houses and the golf course built on the silted-up head of the loch itself. Here the route is rejoined by the walkers' path (NR 937503) virtually opposite Lochranza Field Studies Centre.

For the walker, having waved the main road goodbye in North Glen Sannox, the first step is to follow the minor road down to the picnic place at North Sannox, where the river enters the sea. A quiet and pleasant place this, except of a summer evening when it becomes one of the main feeding grounds of the fearsome Arran midge. From here, follow the track over the stile and along the coast to the north-west. At first, the hillslopes dropping to the coast are clad in trees, but soon these give way to steep heather-covered slopes. After about 2 km, the way appears to be blocked by a fantastic jumble of huge blocks of rock. These 'Fallen Rocks' (NS 004483) are the result of a collapse of the hillside, some say as a result of an earthquake. The path winds through the blocks, beyond which it continues along the shore of one of the loneliest parts of Arran. There are views out across the Firth of Clyde to Bute, the Cowal Peninsula and Kintyre, but on the landward side there are just steep bare hills completely cutting off any prospect of the inhabited part of Arran. Continue along the coast until a solitary habitation, the cottage at Laggan (NR 979508), is reached. No-one lives here permanently now, but the building is kept in quite good repair.

From Laggan, a choice of routes is available. A walk along the shore northwards leads past the old salt pans, where local coal was used to evaporate seawater to produce salt, past the Cock of Arran (NR 956523), a block of rock thought from some angles to resemble a crowing cock, to the difficult terrain of An Scriodain (NR 948523), where rockfalls and slipped masses of rock very like the Fallen Rocks encountered earlier have to be negotiated. After proceeding carefully through these rocks, the way is then open for the geologist to visit one of the most famous sites in the history of the science, Hutton's Unconformity (NR 934519). Here, the juxtaposition of rock layers of different types at varying attitudes led James Hutton in 1787 to deduce that there had been past cycles of change during the development of the modern landscape. From here, the path along the foreshore should be followed to where it joins the main road in the village of Lochranza.

Alternatively, from Laggan, a steep but clearly-marked track leads up and over the hills directly towards Lochranza, passing the ruins of Cock Farm (NR 965512), abandoned finally in 1912. The highest point of this track provides massive vistas over the Firth of Clyde and southwards to the Arran mountains. The track provides an easy walk down through heather and meadow to join the shore route from Laggan at the head of Loch Ranza.

Lochranza village itself is so tightly tucked in beneath the sheltering hills that it is probably the spot that receives the least sunshine in the entire island. Its main claim to fame, though, is the castle (NR 933507), perched on a spit protruding into the bay. The castle, a royal hunting lodge, is possibly of the thirteenth or fourteenth century, at least in parts. It is kept locked, but a plaque gives instructions about where the key may be obtained should you want to explore further.

North from the castle, the route passes the ruins of Lochranza pier, long closed but finally damaged in a storm in 1989, and beside it, the slipway down which cars are loaded onto the ferry that plies the route to Claonaig in Kintyre, at least during the summer months. Beyond the pier, the road starts to turn south, along the west coast of Arran. It runs along the raised beach surface to the little settlement of Catacol, where it is worth stopping for a brief look at the 'Twelve Apostles' (NR 911497), former estate cottages built in the nineteenth century to house those put off the land by clearances in Glen Catacol.

Glen Catacol itself is a splendidly dramatic sight from the road, but those of a botanic bent should make the effort to follow the track on the north side of the glen up to where a nature reserve has been established around a small gorge in which the rare Arran service trees (*sorbus sp.*) are to be found. There is a better-looking path on the south side of the glen, but it is deceptive as it soon peters out, and the walker is left to try and find a way to cross the Catacol Burn, not always an easy task.

Southward from Catacol Bay, the road is squeezed ever more tightly between the shore and the hills, forcing some sharp climbs and rather abrupt crossings of humps in the road. In the midst of all this wildness is a little graveyard by the roadside (NR 884476). It is not known which church this graveyard served, as it is isolated from any of the local settlements.

The route, still following the road, keeps to the low ground of the raised beach as it passes the clachan of Mid Thundergay (NR 882477) perched atop the old cliffline. The energetic should note that this point is the start of a good path up to Coire Fhionn Lochan, the prettiest of the Arran lochs, set in a bowl in the hills and fringed by clean gravel beaches. It is only 3 km from the road, and a visit with a picnic lunch, on a warm day, can be idyllic.

Back on the main road, the route passes through the village of Pirnmill, noted mainly for the remains of the old bobbin or 'pirn' mill which gave it its name. The remains of the mill are beside the stream just behind the present-day post office (NR 873441). From Pirnmill, the route continues southwards through Whitefarland with its sandy beach and palm trees, before climbing towards the cluster of houses that is Imachar (NR 865405). From up here, extensive views both up and down the Kilbrannan Sound give ample opportunity to note the passage of fishing boats between Campbeltown and Tarbert. The route then descends abruptly back almost to beach level, where it stays as it goes past Dougrie Lodge (NR884373), a splendid shooting lodge built beside the Iorsa Water on a site with excellent views of the Arran peaks. The walled gardens here have been opened to the public on occasion in recent years, and are worth a visit should the opportunity arise.

From Dougrie, the route follows the road southwards to Machrie, hugging the raised beach all the way. From here the return to Brodick can be made by way of the minor road which branches from the main road here (NR 892347), and the String Road, a route described in Excursion 4.

EXCURSION 6

A Walk on the Wild Side

This excursion is designed to introduce the visitor to the atmosphere and scenery of the Arran mountains, as spectacular a range of hills as can be found in Scotland. The route described here is exclusively for walkers, and should not be undertaken without at least a basic level of equipment, in particular sturdy footwear and the facility to carry warm clothing, for even on the warmest summer days winds at altitude can soon chill the unwary and ill-prepared walker. However, provided suitable care is taken, this route can be undertaken in safety by anyone who is moderately fit.

The starting point is the foot of the String Road where it branches off from the main road round the island just outside Brodick (NS 005368). Walk up the String Road for about 80 m, and then turn right along a minor road signposted to Glen Rosa (NS 003368). This road should be followed across the bridge over the Shurig Burn and along past the riding stables, ignoring the branch track on the left (west), which leads into Glen Shurig. After following the metalled road as far as Glenrosa Farm (NS 001376) the route passes through a gateway and becomes a rough track soon afterwards. The deteriorating conditions underfoot are more than compensated for by the view that opens up as the track is followed into Glen Rosa. Here, the sweep of the lower glen leads the eye up towards the peaks of Ben Nuis (the triangular one at the south [left] end of the ridge) and Beinn Tarsuinn, with a shoulder of Beinn a' Chliabhainn coming into view. The track is followed through the deer fence (negotiated by means of a small gateway) and over a muddy section of ground before rising gently to give a view of the lower glen (NR 989380). The large lumps or mounds on the floor of the valley are moraines, masses of sediment left behind by the glaciers which occupied the glen about 10,500 years ago.

The route continues past the moraines and the 'bridge' over the Rosa formed by the pipeline constructed to carry water from the Garbh Allt, a tributary of the Rosa, to Brodick. As a

The heavy usage of some of the more popular footpaths in Arran has resulted in their becoming eroded and difficult to walk along. In Glen Rosa a troop of workers has been employed to repair and improve a footpath used by hundreds, if not thousands, of visitors every year.

curve in the glen is rounded, a still more impressive vista opens up. Directly ahead is the conical peak called Cir Mhor (NR 973432), dominating the glen. Just visible over the right shoulder of Cir Mhor are two towers separated by a deep gash. This is the 'Witches Step' (NR 977444), formed by the weathering out of a dyke of weak rock which cuts across the harder granite. To right and left of Glen Rosa great slopes rise steeply skywards, exposing large slabs of bare rock, the slabs on the right being topped by the distant peak of Goatfell (NR 991415). The whole impression is one of grandeur, but on a scale that is not intimidating. These hills seem to welcome the visitor rather than raise defences against him.

The track deteriorates again at the bridge over the Garbh Allt (NR 982387), a tributary of the Rosa that comes rushing down the flanks of Glen Rosa in a welter of waterfalls, pools and chutes where the water pours over great slabs of granite. Walkers looking for just a sample of the Arran mountains will

A competitor in the annual Goatfell race reaches the summit. The race, held every May, attracts runners from all over Scotland as well as some from south of the Border.

often use the bridge as their turning point and will then retrace their steps to Brodick. The track beyond this point, while quite clear, used to be very wet indeed, sometimes degenerating into a quagmire negotiated by jumping from boulder to boulder. Nowadays, thanks to the work of groups of volunteers, there is a much improved path for at least a kilometre or so beyond the bridge, and most people should now be able to travel a fair distance up the glen without getting their feet wet.

Once the made path ends, the going becomes rather less easy, but providing common sense is used the worst of the wet can be avoided. One tip is to keep close to the river — it seems to be slightly drier there, and the walker can also then take full advantage of one of the most attractive streams on the island. The Rosa is a constant delight, tumbling as small waterfalls into narrow gorges, flowing as a thin curtain of crystal-clear water over slabs of granite on which sunbathing can be most agreeable in suitable weather, and providing a source of cooling water for the slaking of thirsts. The hills become ever more impressive as the route draws closer to them, and the peaks seem to float far above the walker, with buzzards, ravens or eagles sometimes soaring around them.

The route crosses the main branch of the Rosa at a point where the glen opens out (NR 978415). The actual crossing is not too hazardous, though it can become quite exciting if the river happens to be in spate. Once across this obstacle, the path heads upslope towards the Saddle (NR 978432), a pass just to the right (east) of the shapely peak of Cir Mhor. If the gradient of the path strains the lungs a bit, then the view of the surrounding cliffs and crags, with the trough of Glen Rosa stretching away back towards Brodick, soon refreshes. The summit of the Saddle is reached, to reveal a view even more spectacular than those already encountered. The view of Glen Sannox, on the far side of the pass, provides an even more dramatic mountain landscape than that of Glen Rosa. Facing across the glen, the gash of the Witches Step rears into the sky, while to its left a series of great granite towers crowns the peak commonly called The Castles (NR 969444), the second highest summit in Arran. The near side of the glen is similarly steep and smoothed by the passage of ice in bygone eras, while framed between the peaks guarding the entrance to the glen the waters of the Firth of Clyde can be seen, with the Isle of Bute visible in the distance.

From the Saddle a choice of routes is available. The sturdy walker may be interested in including the capture of the summit of Goatfell in the day's excursion, while those content to remain at lower altitudes can descend into Glen Sannox and return to the main road at Sannox itself. The actual descent from the Saddle into the glen is steep, and care needs to be taken, especially over the first 30 m or so of the descent. Immediately below the Saddle, crags guard the descent to Glen Sannox, but by taking a route at the left-hand (western) end of the crags, a short natural staircase leads to easier terrain below. The easiest way to locate this routeway is to look for boot scratches on the rocks, and to follow these downwards.

Once the floor of Glen Sannox is reached, paths follow both sides of the burn down towards the mouth of the glen. Neither path is very good, and the walker is likely again to have to make detours around boggy terrain, but the south (right) side of the burn is the one to be on by the time it emerges from the narrow confines of the mountains. The views back up the glen from here are spectacular, though slightly spoiled by the ruins of the old barytes mill (NS 009452). Passing the ruins, the path soon improves to a track which returns to the main road at a point where transport can be obtained back to Brodick.

For the more adventurous walker, the route from the Saddle lies not down but up, along the ridge rising to the east towards Goatfell. With the climb, in reality a steep walk made more tiring by having to cross areas of granite gravel which roll away beneath the soles of the boots, the view continues to expand. At the top of the ridge, the peak of North Goat Fell offers great expanses of landscape to gaze upon, as most of the upper Firth of Clyde is now open to view, while to the west, beyond Arran, the hills of Islay and Jura rise skywards.

The route now lies southwards along the ridge to the summit of Goatfell itself. The ridge is blocked by a series of granite towers which provide some amusing scrambling, although amusement is likely to turn into something else if you get too far onto the western side of any of these crags, where you will feel as though you are hanging in mid-air over Glen Rosa. An easier path runs across the turf-covered slopes to the east and just below the ridge crest, rising to regain the crest just before the rounded summit of Goatfell is reached. On a good day it is worth lingering to try and make out details of the huge vista, one of the finest in Scotland. It is said that the Glencoe hills, possibly Ben Nevis, peaks in Donegal and the Mountains of Mourne, the Isle of Man and the spire of Glasgow Cathedral can be seen in suitable conditions.

Once the sightseeing is complete, the route lies down the ridge on the east side of the mountain, towards Corrie. Take care to keep to the right of any crags on the descent. At about 600 m there is a fork, the left-hand route leading steeply down to the coast at Corrie, while the right-hand trail leads across gentle moorland and down into the woods of the policies of Brodick Castle, eventually regaining the main road at Cladach (NS 012377).

Further Reading

The Arran Naturalist. Journal of the Arran Natural History Society. Brodick.

Balfour, J.A. (ed). *The Book of Arran,* Glasgow, 1910.

Bryce, J. *Geology of Clydesdale and Arran.* Glasgow, 1859.

Currie, R. *The Place-Names of Arran.* Glasgow, 1908.

Fairhurst, H. *Exploring Arran's Past.* Brodick, 1982.

Johnstone, J.M. *Rock Climbs in Arran.* Scottish Mountaineering Club, Edinburgh, 1958.

Landsborough, D. *Excursions to Arran, with reference to the Natural History of the Island.* Edinburgh. 1847.

MacGregor, M. *Excursion Guide to the Geology of Arran.* Geological Society of Glasgow, 1983.

MacKenzie, W.M. (ed), *The Book of Arran,* vol. 2. Glasgow, 1914.

McLellan, R. *Ancient Monuments of Arran. Official Guide.* H.M.S.O. Edinburgh, 1977.

McLellan, R. *The Isle of Arran,* 3rd edition. London, 1985.

Ramsay, A. *The Geology of the Island of Arran from Original Survey.* Glasgow, 1841.

Scottish Women's Rural Institute, Arran. *History of the Villages of the Isle of Arran,* 1983.

Storrie, M.C. and Jackson, C.I. *Arran 1980-81: 2021?* Scottish Council of Social Service, Edinburgh, 1967.

The Third Statistical Account of Scotland, vol. XI. Glasgow, 1962.

Tomkeieff, S.I. Geologists' Association Guide No. 32, *Isle of Arran.* Colchester, 1961.

Tyrrell, G.W. *The Geology of Arran.* Memoir of the Geological Survey. Edinburgh, 1928.

Whittow, J.B. *Geology and Scenery in Scotland.* Penguin Books, 1977.

Index